THE LITTLE
PLATOONS

THE LITTLE PLATOONS

Sub-Local Governments in Modern History

GEORGE W. LIEBMANN

PRAEGER

Westport, Connecticut
London

Library of Congress Cataloging-in-Publication Data

Liebmann, George W.
   The little platoons : sub-local governments in modern history /
George W. Liebmann.
      p.   cm.
   Includes bibliographical references and indexes.
   ISBN 0–275–95178–2 (alk. paper)
   1. Decentralization in government.   2. Local government.
3. Political participation.   I. Title.
JS113.L54   1995
320.8—dc20   95–5308

British Library Cataloguing in Publication Data is available.

Library of Congress Catalog Card Number: 95–5308
ISBN: 0–275–95178–2

First published in 1995

Praeger Publishers, 88 Post Road West, Westport, CT 06881
An imprint of Greenwood Publishing Group, Inc.

Printed in the United States of America

The paper used in this book complies with the
Permanent Paper Standard issued by the National
Information Standards Organization (Z39.48–1984).

10 9 8 7 6 5 4 3 2 1

For Anne-Lise

The liberal age could give its whole attention to the propagation of the idea of freedom, for it could build on the foundations of the traditional conformity it had inherited from the old community culture of the Middle Ages. We shall have to waste a great deal of energy in the next few years replacing the old pattern of traditional conformity which is now disintegrating by a new one. . . . The mere fact of the existence of masses is no obstacle. . . . In small groups in which everyone feels that a great deal depends upon his actions, and learns to act upon his own responsibility instead of losing himself in the anonymity of the mass, social patterns grow up in which individuality can almost certainly develop.

--Karl Mannheim

There is no lack of schemes for the regeneration of society, schemes not infrequently of a sort which would not be needed by a society capable of freely adopting them. The construction of a theoretical paradise is the easiest of human efforts. The familiar method is to establish the perfect or almost perfect state, and then to fashion human beings to fit it. This is a far lighter undertaking than the necessary and unspectacular task, taking human nature as it is and is likely to remain, of contriving improvements that are workable.

--Charles Evans Hughes

There is nothing more insidious than the notion that big, rapid changes are easier or more fruitful than small, slow changes; it leads to talk without action, to action without talk, and perhaps to collapse of democracy under a mass of accumulated, neglected routine business. The way to multiply big problems is to neglect small ones. There is nothing seriously wrong with our institutional system save our proclivity to waste time attacking or defending it and to neglect proper tasks of changing it continuously by wise collective experimentation.

--Henry Simons

Contents

Preface

One who writes a book on a hitherto unfamiliar subject--the comparison of community-level governments in seven major countries--perhaps owes the world some explanation.

My interest in these matters arose from a casual conversation with a German friend who remarked on the inconvenience of life in the suburban United States, including the absence of "mother-in-law" apartments and convenience stores. This led to a series of articles in American Bar Association publications, the first on the question of mixed uses in suburban zoning, the second on the detrimental effects of many land use controls on both community and the environment, and the third on the developing phenomenon of the residential community association and its possible use to remedy both legal and social deficits in the United States.

At about the same time, I had read much of the recent political science literature deploring the decline of civil society in the West and expanding on the need for a revival of communitarian institutions. This body of writing seemed to me to be long on exhortation and short on illustrations of how these aspirations might be realized. Hence, the present book, written while I was a Simon Industrial and Professional Fellow at the University of Manchester.

The premise of the work is that the growing centralization of government, though popularly viewed as an inevitable result of advances in transportation and communications and the need to relieve feudal inequities, has itself generated problems that can only be relieved through a partial return to older forms of social organization. This is true for two reasons:

First, the vaunted advances in mobility have done little to change the situation of the very young, the very old, and their caretakers, who remain rooted and indeed isolated in their neighborhoods. If services are to be provided to an ever-growing older population, and the young made part of a culture, mutual aid and neighborhood organization are essential, as is increasingly recognized in the practice of both authoritarian and democratic states.

Second, a political regime that accords legitimacy only to the individual as a market actor and to the national state erodes civic virtues essential both to effective economic functioning and to the maintenance of free government; in that sense, as writers like Niebuhr and Schumpeter suggested, the modern capitalist state rests on precapitalist foundations. An obscure and recently republished book of Walter Lippmann, *The Phantom Public*, speaks directly to this question in terms that modern Americans at least will find recognizable:

A century ago, the model of popular government was the self-sufficient township in which the voters' opinions were formed and corrected by talk with their neighbors--under absentee government, these checks upon opinions are lacking. The consequences are often so remote and long-delayed that error is not promptly disclosed. In the interdependent world, desire, rather than custom or objective law, tends to become the criterion of men's conduct. They formulate their demands at large for "security" at the expense of everyone else's safety, for "morality" at the expense of other men's tastes and comfort, for a fulfillment of a national destiny that consists of taking what you want when you want it. The lengthening of the interval between conduct and experience, between cause and effect, has nurtured a cult of self-expression in which each thinker thinks about his own thoughts and has subtle feelings about his feelings. That he does not in consequence deeply affect the course of affairs is not surprising.[1]

A more contemporary commentator, Peter Riesenberg, has similarly noted:

[T]he institutions that ancient and medieval citizens depended on . . . do not work too well for us. Our churches no longer help shape a common morality as a basis for politics; often they provide the issues for a violent politics. Our schools are too confused in their method and methodology to do anything but attempt to teach basic skills and retail the most traditional and ineffectual civics. With about fourteen million Americans working for some government, public service has become a job and hardly serves as the education for, or means to, virtue.[2]

The present writer cannot join with Riesenberg in deploring the rise among "the affluent and well educated" of "their private world of clubs, schools, and self-policed neighborhoods" nor in concluding that the ordinary citizen can find "the path to virtue" only in "altruistic service in the private sector, and perhaps in occasional office-holding at the level of local government as well." This book is intended as a demonstration that modern societies, at times and in places, have done better than that, by seeking to make available to the population at large such "private worlds," whose methods are small-scale governments, street associations, self-governing schools, community care, neighborhood publications, and the purposeful strengthening of the remnants of traditional institutions.

Many have expressed concern on social equity grounds with the fate of poorer neighborhoods if an increasing array of public services are delivered by small associations and more political support is consequently withdrawn from local government. In one sense, these concerns are well founded, less by reason of differences in economic wealth and more by reason of the fact that American law generally denies established neighborhoods means of organization comparable to community associations. This deficit is beginning to be remedied, through both the conversion of rental properties into condominium regimes and the organization of historic, special, and business improvement districts. Much, however, remains to be done to facilitate the organization of *woonerfs*, street associations, and like entities and to empower tenants in rental housing.

With the larger criticism, that proceeding from economic equity, the author has more limited sympathy. The existing infrastructure and surplus housing stock of American inner cities and the transfer payments into them, when compared with those of viable neighborhoods in other nations, both advanced and underdeveloped, are such as to indicate that the real deficits are social more than economic. As Durkheim observed:

Average comfort has increased on all levels of the social hierarchy, although perhaps not always in equal proportions. The maladjustment from which we suffer . . . bears witness not to greater economic poverty, but to an alarming poverty of morality .
While the State becomes inflated and hypertrophied in order to obtain a firm enough grip upon individuals, but without succeeding, the latter, without mutual relationships, tumble over one another like so many liquid molecules.[3]

In their description of practices, the chapters forswear depiction of the local and experimental, on the one hand, and those inspired by the fervor of total war, on the other; the test for inclusion is that of acceptance in a major nation for an extended period.

I am indebted to my sponsors for the Simon Fellowship, Prof. Mary Ann Glendon of the Harvard Law School, my former law partner Robert G. Levy, and John McInespie of Glasgow. For numerous courtesies while in Manchester, I am indebted to Prof. P. M. A. Broda, warden of Broomcroft House to whom I owe a special debt for both his interest in the project and for providing an ideal work environment; Dean Rodney Brazier and Prof. Martin Loughlin of the Faculty of Law; and Jeffrey Brider of the Simon Fellowship Committee. My associate, Orbie R. Shively, and my secretary, Jeanette I. Scott, rendered indispensable help in the preparation and review of the manuscript.

NOTES

1. W. Lippmann, *The Phantom Public* (1925), at 181-83.

2. P. Riesenberg, *Citizenship in the Western Tradition: Plato to Rousseau* (1992), at x-xi.

3. E. Durkheim, *Suicide* (1952), at 386-87, 389.

THE LITTLE PLATOONS

1

Britain—The Vestiges of Parochial Administration

The British rural villager, though in myth a self-governing citizen, in fact possesses few powers of self-government. Most important among these are the powers conferred by the 1988 Education Act permitting the parents of each school to elect school governors. Since 1944, parish councils have had the right to select a single member of elementary school boards of governors, but parish powers have otherwise been reduced to the trivial--the maintenance of footpaths and bus shelters, allotments, village streetlighting and playing fields, and the opportunity to comment on planning applications. Recent proposals for the revival of parish constables contemplate applications for funds to central government. No major public service is funded or administered at the village level, though the survival of parish councils makes further development possible. The two levels of local government above the parish level are in the process of being consolidated into one, and limitations on the taxing powers of local governments--so-called rate capping--have subordinated all British local governments to the center, although a reaction against this process has recently set in.

The city dweller in England is in an even worse predicament so far as participation in government is concerned. While his Scottish counterpart elects community councils, in England, except for a few historic parishes, there is no equivalent. In London, there is no citywide municipal government, and borough governments each include several hundred thousand people. There are recent movements to give tenants in council housing and in enfranchised leaseholds powers to govern their buildings, but with these exceptions, and those provided by school governors, local government for British city dwellers is remote indeed.

In Britain, once thought of as a bastion of local liberties, the drastic decline in the importance of traditional local institutions, which began in the 1830s as a reaction against their control by local oligarchies, has yet to fully reverse itself. The reaction against centralization has been a reaction in favor of the private sector, which has not yet translated itself into a revival of local and sub-local institutions.

Of the nations considered, Britain has the longest history of parochial or neighborhood administration. The rise of the state and the centralization induced by its intense mobilization in the 1939-45 war--a mobilization more intensive even than that of Germany and Russia--have withered its local institutions. The reaction against centralization in the Thatcher years gave rise to enthusiasm for deregulation, privatization, and market institutions, at the further expense of the mediating structures of local government. The traditional theory of the English Constitution--"the powers of the local authorities in Britain belong to a residual domain preserved by the local authorities as their legitimate and traditional terrain against enactments from the centre"[1]--is scarcely descriptive of present conditions.

Yet parish institutions survive, at least in rural areas, and a Conservative government has been driven by its own market logic toward the creation of new communal groupings at the building and housing project level that may in time suspiciously resemble urban parishes. The prospect for revival of miniature government is considerable since in England, unlike the United States, party competition has operated to refute Tocqueville's proposition that "the only public men in democracies who favor decentralization are, almost invariably, either very disinterested or extremely mediocre; the former are scarce and the latter powerless."[2] The opposition parties have frequently been driven, in administering local councils under their control, to follow the logic of a recent French commentator.

[C]ritics of the current centralizing tendency may well find that the only alternative ideological defense is a revival of notions of community and participation despite the evidence [based on current large local districts] that they appear to have little to link them. Such participatory communities would possibly be at levels rather smaller than the present local government authorities which are so much under attack.[3]

ORIGINS OF THE PARISH

The parish dates from the age of manorial government when "the opportunities presented by the periodical gatherings of the parish under the guidance of the parish priest were taken for the discussion and transaction of secular business of common interest, away from the unpopular and tyrannous court of the manor."[4]

ROADS

With the collapse of manorial government in the fourteenth century, the parish increasingly assumed civil functions, notably for highway maintenance and poor relief, the evolution of which is vividly, if unsympathetically, described in Sidney and Beatrice Webb's *The Development of English Local Government*. By a statute of 1555,[5] "the obligation to provide for maintenance of all public highways rested on the parish as a whole and on every inhabitant thereof," who was required to provide or supply labor for work on the roads under the direction of a parish surveyor. By 1563, six days' annual service was required. The theoretical obligation of personal service on roads lasted until 1835, having been repealed in Ireland in 1762 and in France in 1764. As late as 1920 the Webbs could write that "it still exists for the maintenance of roads outside the cities in all but five of the United States."[6] In explaining the demise of the obligation of service, the Webbs observe, in language pertinent to all efforts at participatory neighborhood or miniature government, that "when the relative equality of conditions of the medieval manor was left behind, the burden imposed by the law was seen to be very unevenly distributed."[7] By 1654, the parish was permitted to provide for road upkeep through the rates, a provision confirmed by the Restoration Parliament in 1662. In 1670, parishioners were permitted to make payments in lieu of service, a fatal breach in the theory of the system, as was later shown in the history of watch committees for law enforcement and indeed in America's civil war conscription law. It was thus observed that "one hired team is almost if not quite equal to two duty teams with regard to the work done in a day," and the laborers were referred to as "the King's loiterers." In the year before repeal, in 1835, the system was said to be "a mere farce and a farce attended by false pretense." Yet the system was defended in agricultural districts because of its frugality and because all that was wanted was not highway improvement but "the maintenance of some imaginary status quo."[8] Although service in kind was abolished in 1835 and the creation of District Highway Boards was authorized, resistance to expenditure ensured that as late as 1882, 6,203 parishes still maintained responsibility for road maintenance. Parochial road maintenance was definitively abolished and transferred to Rural Sanitary Authorities by the Local Government Act of 1894, though the parishes retain to this day responsibility for maintenance of footpaths other than those along rights of way and a veto over stopping up or closing of roads.

POOR RELIEF

The displacement of the parishes in poor law administration by the Poor Law Amendment Act of 1834[9] took place almost at the same time as the abolition of the road service system. Poor relief became a parish, as distinct from a church, function in 1563. In 1723,[10] as a result of the incapacity of smaller parishes to maintain poor houses and workhouses, Parliament authorized the contracting out of workhouses.[11]

The farming of the workhouse, on genuinely commercial principles, inevitably prevented its use either as a deterrent or as a place of salutary regimen. The more numerous its inmates, the larger (assuming payment per head) was the contractor's income, and the more certain his profit. It was therefore to his interest to make the house as attractive as he could to the pauper class, and especially to such as were able-bodied; and this he could most cheaply and most certainly do by allowing personal freedom. Naturally it never occurred to the contractor to run his establishment in such a way as to educate or reform the paupers, a duty for which he was not engaged or paid.[12]

Beginning in 1662, any person not in possession of a specified amount of property was subject to being returned to the parish of his origin, whether or not he sought poor relief. This law was described as making "the most effectual and extensive invasion of the rights of Englishmen which had ever been attempted since the Conquest."[13] This law was restricted in 1795 to more limited classes of persons, rogues, vagrants, unmarried mothers, and persons seeking poor relief. With the development of industry, parish officers resorted "to the evasion of pushing the vagrant, or the incomer across the parish boundary."[14] Hence came into being the Poor Law Amendment Act, with its establishment of unions of parishes and its premise that "the pauper must not be pampered in one union and starved in another. Every statutory or administrative rule should be rigidly carried out in every part of the Kingdom."[15]

The parish as a governmental institution was almost sent to its demise in 1834. The elimination of the parish poor rate left the

[u]ncontrolled and unlimited Church Rate, by long tradition applicable to all the other purposes of parochial government, and levied by the popularly elected churchwardens. It so chanced that just at this period, the nonconformist majority dominating the Open Vestries in the large industrial towns--forgetting both the past history and the contemporary utility of the parish vestry and the powers that it wielded--unwittingly threw away, by steadfastly voting against anything called a Church Rate, the immemorial right of the inhabitants in vestry assembled to tax themselves for any purpose of public utility. . . . [T]he parish as a unit of local government in the England outside the Metropolitan area came virtually to an end.[16]

LAW ENFORCEMENT

At about the same time, the parish and communal role in law enforcement began its decline, with the London Police Act of 1829 and the statute of 1856 requiring all English counties to maintain professional police forces. The mandate of the Statute of Winchester[17] requiring a watch drawn from the citizenry and that "such as keep the town shall follow with hue and cry with all the town" likewise fell into desuetude, as did, with less justification, a latter-day version of the hue and cry--the publication of broadsides containing descriptions of wanted criminals. "Professional bureaucratic policing as it developed in England was not reconciled with the kind of public participation that had underpinned the success of the eighteenth-century crime advertisement."[18] The vestigial right of parishes to appoint constables was eliminated in 1964.

THE MODERN PARISH

The Local Government Act of 1858 interrupted the progress of centralization by allowing meetings of ratepayers in local subdivisions to choose by two-thirds vote to assume local jurisdiction over a wide array of enumerated functions and even to establish (with the acquiescence of the Home Secretary) new local subdivisions. This permissive legislation was described by Disraeli in 1875 as "the characteristic of a free people. It is easy to adopt compulsory legislation when you have to deal with those who only exist to obey, but in a free country, and especially in a country like England, you must trust to persuasion and example as the two great elements, if you wish to effect any considerable change in the manners and customs of the people."[19]

As late as 1981, there were 14,926 civil parishes in England and Wales, of which 13,093 were in rural areas. Approximately 6,000 of the rural parishes had populations of less than 300.[20] In 1894, a Parish Council Act passed by a Liberal government[21] vested the powers of the parish in parish meetings consisting of all the electors of the parish. In 1883, a bill prepared by Sir Charles Dilke to strengthen parishes had failed to be enacted due to other priorities. In 1888, a Conservative government sponsored a Local Government Act, vesting powers in county councils, which Dilke and others criticized on the basis that "there was no building upon of the smaller districts . . . where the people were at their homes."[22] Others urged strengthening of the parish on the basis that

[t]he county was too large an area to arouse the interest of the agricultural laborer or to enable him to take his part in local administration. . . . If the parish were equipped

with a proper governing body, it would be a suitable unit for dealing with problems that affected the ordinary villager--the management of the schoolroom and its letting for meetings, the village water supply, allotments, parochial charities.[23]

An amendment in this sense was defeated; however, upon the return of the Liberals to power, the powers of parishes were finally enlarged. "The argument resolved itself into a discussion between those who favored a small unit, where the ordinary laborer could attend to local government work within his own neighborhood, and those preferring the bigger area just because it meant that only persons with more leisure could travel to the district center to transact administrative business."[24]

The proposal to vest direct powers of government in parish meetings was denounced by some Conservatives as an intrusion on representative government and as opening the door to a plebiscite or referendum. Others, including Dilke and some Conservatives, sought to raise from 200 to a higher number the threshold at which parishes might choose councils--the Radicals out of regard for direct democracy, the Conservatives out of a desire not to create official bodies competitive with county councils.[25] In the final event, the parishes were given most of the nonecclesiastical powers previously exercised by the Vestry, except that the vestigial highway boards were abolished.[26] The parish was given the power to appeal against tax assessments and to manage all vestry property not held for ecclesiastical charters, including village greens and allotments. In addition, the parish was given limited powers to drain and cover pools and utilize wells and springs where it could do so without interfering with private rights or those of any public authority. It also was accorded certain rights to complain and to exercise delegated powers.[27]

In addition, parishes were accorded the right to repair footpaths, other than those along public roads, and to withhold consent from proposed highway diversions.[28] Finally, parishes were allowed to acquire land by purchase for rights of way and recreation grounds, to let allotments, to seek the aid of the County Council with respect to compulsory purchase of land, and to adopt responsibilities under certain acts relating to street lighting and public libraries.[29]

The fiscal powers of parish councils included the power with the consent of the parish meeting to levy a rate "of sixpence on the pound on the rateable value of the parish" (i.e., 2.5% of rateable value) or half that amount where the consent of the parish meeting is not obtained. Parish council parishes, in addition, could levy rates to defer expenses under adoptive acts, such as that for streetlighting.[30]

By 1899, 7,076 of the 7,384 council parishes had some expenditures. The major items of expenditure were for lighting, burial grounds, and allotments, the latter being offset by rentals.

By the Education Act of 1902, parishes were permitted to appoint one manager in six for voluntary schools, a provision continued with respect to all primary schools by the Education Act of 1944. Later, as a result of recommendations of the Taylor Committee in 1977, a parent representative was added to each board. More recently, the Education Reform Act of 1988, sec. 40, provided for drastic decentralization of the control of education. While the boards of local authority schools continue to be composed as before under the Education (No. 2) Act of 1986, and must include specified proportions of parents, teachers, local education authority appointees and co-opted governors, the powers of the governors now extend to automatic receipt of a budget share and "to spending any sum . . . as they think fit for the purposes of the school." In addition, if a school opts out from local authority control, its governing body must include at least five parent governors, one or two teacher governors, the head teacher, and co-opted governors outnumbering the other governors, at least two of whom must be parents, and the school will receive direct grants from central government. These changes "have enfranchised parents and created a quarter million army of school governors" though prompted by "a strategy of central control which needed local agents in the drive against local education authorities and professional interest."

In 1949, the parish was made responsible for preparing maps of footpaths under the National Parks and Access to the Countryside Act 1949. The Parish Councils Act of 1957, enacted by a Conservative government, further widened parochial authority by eliminating the need for formal adoption of the 1833 Lighting Act and the Public Improvement Act of 1860 (relating to provision of seats in public places) in order for parishes to exercise powers under them. The act, in addition, contained authority to provide bus shelters, public clocks, and parking places for bicycles and motor vehicles and to contribute to the maintenance of burial grounds and war memorials and relieved parishes of the need for council approval of borrowing.

In 1966, a Labour government appointed a Royal Commission on Local Government in England and a corresponding commission for Scotland. The Local Government (Miscellaneous Provisions) Act of 1963 had allowed parish councils to assess a rate of 1.5p on the pound for miscellaneous uses. The Memorandum of Evidence of the Parish Councils Association indicated that some 90 activities not legally possible previously had been engaged in, including creation of car pools; resurfacing of roads or markets; installation of public lavatories, public telephones, and village surgeries; repairs to old buildings; junk disposal; prizes; association memberships; civic entertainments; fencing; provision of a road warden and first-aid post; signs, maps, and handbooks; sponsorship of play groups and theater groups; ambulances; meals on wheels; day nurseries; mobile physiotherapy and marriage guidance services; flower shows;

restocking of streams; trusteeships of disused fire stations; and provision of musical instruments for a band.[31]

The association's statement stressed that "with a parish authority the emphasis is on helping [people] to help themselves. . . . [a]t parish level the statutory and the voluntary are locked in a close embrace."[32] "[M]uch of their effectiveness can be judged not from the business they have in hand or the money they spend but by the influence or leverage they can exert." At that time, parish councils had approximately 1,800 full-time employees, a majority of them groundsmen, cemetery keepers, and caretakers.[33] This compares with approximately 600,000 central government and 1.8 million local authority employees in England in 1981.[34]

The statement further noted "that the average or median age of parish counsellors has fallen a long way since 1948 and that the proportion of women has risen and continues to do so [and] is now [1966] about 20%."[35] At many county meetings of parish counselors, the National Association's representatives have taken counts among those present. The percentage of those living in their native parish never rises on those occasions above 30%, and falls to as low as 10% in areas close to a big city. Collective voluntary activity has therefore, to thrive at all, to be organized in a more formal and self-conscious fashion than hitherto."[36] The statement alludes to old people's welfare committees and nursery schools and creches as "this voluntary system which, with parish council stiffening, is the cheapest method of administration ever devised, and by no means the least efficient." The association sought "relax[ation] of the doctrine of ultra vires . . . empowering the village authorities to spend funds at their discretion for the benefit of their own inhabitants, leaving it to the necessities of economics and the limitations on total expenditure to set limits to their activities."[37] The Association further sought notice of planning, housing, and highway applications. "The village . . . has something, namely local knowledge, to give."[38] Further, "[i]t is important that the representatives of grassroots democracy should have something to do as well as something to say. They must have real, if local, power because nothing else will ensure a responsible attitude toward public affairs." A contemporary account observed that "led by the articulate and humorous Professor Bryan Keith-Lucas, the [Parish Councils] Association provided just about the only interesting session for the handful of members of the public who observed proceedings."[39]

The total expenditures of the parishes in 1963 were stated to be 7.5 million pounds.[40] By 1993, in addition to funds spent on local services, parish councils received 2.9 million pounds for acting as agents for higher levels of government, usually in connection with street cleaning (12% of councils, 34% of those with populations of more than 20,000). Dame Evelyn Sharp, permanent secretary at the Ministry of Housing from 1955 to 1966, had envisaged a greater importance for such delegations of authority: "[The Parish Council] could build the odd houses-for any purpose-and tackle the improvement of older houses. It could look after all the council houses and tenants in its area on behalf of the main authority."[41]

The Royal Commission recommended that the 0.2 pence limit on miscellaneous expenses "should disappear and should not be replaced by any other limit."[42] It further recommended that county councils be empowered to delegate housing, preservation, minor highway, and conservation powers to parish councils. As to metropolitan areas, it recommended that creation of such councils be optional and that councils in metropolitan areas not be authorized to make capital expenditures or accept delegations of main services. An extended dissent by Derek Senior, Esq., favored two tiers of local government above the parish councils, rather than a unitary system, and recommended that parish councils be given a right of notification with respect to plans for physical development in their areas, be elected annually, and (anticipating the thrust of the 1988 Education Act) be empowered to nominate a majority, and not merely one member, of school governing bodies. It alluded to a role for parishes in meals on wheels, home help services, small hostels, and the use of school buildings. Senior stressed participation values: "At this level, direct observation does have some chance to prevail against the cultivated image."[43]

URBAN PARISHES

The companion (Wheatley) Commission on Local Government in Scotland, where parish councils did not exist, recommended that community councils without taxing power be created on application of local communities in urban as well as rural areas with power to improve local amenities and serve as agents for higher levels of government. The government's response was to indicate "a preference for non-statutory consultative bodies rather than a fully developed pattern of neighborhood councils in the larger urban areas."[44] The Local Government (Scotland) Act, 1973, provides that each local authority shall submit a scheme for the establishment of community councils within its area "to ascertain and express views and to take such action as appears to be expedient and practicable." Local authority contributions and loans to community councils are authorized. In Glasgow, Aberdeen, and other major cities, there is a council for every 8,000 to 10,000 persons, which receives small grants from the local authority, typically of about 1,000 pounds annually.

The Local Government Act of 1972, enacted under a Conservative government, provided for two tiers of local government above the parish council, rather than the single tier recommended by the Royal Commission, and accorded parishes the right to be informed of planning applications but limited their rating authority to 2 pence on the pound. While the Labour white paper would have limited councils to advisory functions, the Conservatives gave at least lip service to providing "worthwhile functions" for the "bottom tier." In urban areas outside London, parishes might be established where there was a historic parish (10,200 such parishes were located in urban areas), the population of the parish was not more than one fifth that of the local government district, and the parish population was less than 10,000. Creation was discretionary where parish populations were in the 10,000 to 20,000 range. Only about 300 urban parishes resulted, since there was no authorization of urban parishes in parts of a town. Subsequently, 90 locally organized urban parish councils were formed in Birmingham, a city with a population of about 1 million.

The role of Scottish community councils is said to include the organization of play groups, festivals, and community centers and the designation of members of school councils and local health committees, in addition to youth activities, pensioners' clubs, and information and advice centers.

The 2 pence limit was still a large increase from the old 0.2 pence limit and resulted from an amendment in the House of Lords to the government's proposal for a 0.5 pence limit.

RECENT PROPOSALS FOR THE PARISH

The curtailment of local government powers by the Thatcher government in the 1980s did little to affect parish council powers. The Local Government Act of 1992 subjected parish councils to the Citizens' Charter. The Conservative government resisted demands from opposition parties, including Scottish and Welsh Nationalists, for expanded parish council powers, including the suggestion of Goronwy Daniel that "many voluntary workers are most interested in making their services available close to their own home and within their local community"[45] and that of Philip Abrams that "neighborhood care means working out a constructive relationship between the state, nationally and locally, and neighborhoodism, the politicized voice of local attachment."[46] There has been considerable interest in the concept of community care, beginning with a white paper in 1963, a 1978 discussion document on care for the aging, a 1983 Ministry of Health initiative, later reports of the Audit Commission, and several House of Commons Committees, followed by a major white paper in 1989, enactment of the National Health Service and Community Care Act in 1990, and a 1991 study of community work in the probation service.[47]

The most recent statements of the Conservative government relating to local government in Wales and Scotland do not arrest the movement toward expansion of parish powers but do not accelerate it either. The Welsh statement[48] declares that it "does not propose to diminish their powers and responsibilities in any way. Equally however, it has no wish to reintroduce a two-tier system of local government by adding to their existing powers of service delivery." However, where a Welsh council provides service delivery on an agency basis, "it would be open to the community council if it so wished to enhance the level of service at its own expense." The Scottish statement confined itself to a declaration that the "[g]overnment are examining ways of giving community councils, when those councils request it, greater input into decisions on planning and licensing matters within their immediate areas."[49]

In its submission to the currently sitting Local Government (Banham) Commission, the Conservative government has declared that it "does not believe it would be right to provide across-the-board increases in [parish] rights and duties,"[50] though expressing some willingness to lift restrictions on creation of new parishes for towns with more than 20,000 persons. It is striking that the role now envisaged for parishes by a Conservative government is more restricted than that proposed in 1920 by Sidney and Beatrice Webb in their Constitution for the Socialist Commonwealth of Great Britain, which proposed that existing parishes, "a couple of thousand families in the country and twice or thrice that number in large cities" elect ward councilors, who would superintend particular public services either singly or in committees, depending on the need for centralized administration of a given service.

It may well be, for instance, that paving, lighting and cleansing the thoroughfares, the prevention of nuisances, the management of elementary schools and the provision of public baths and washhouses are best administered together for a group of neighbors resident within a comparatively small area. On the other hand . . . water supply, the tramway service, electricity, . . . parks, town planning, . . . and university education call for areas of much greater magnitude. . . . Each Ward . . . would necessarily become, not only an electoral unit, but also a unit for the collection of rates or local taxes.[51]

HOUSING BLOCK COMMUNITIES

In a different sphere, however, that of urban housing projects and blocks, the present government has been led into fostering several new forms of local or collective unit. The Conservative Manifesto in 1987 declared:

We will give groups of tenants the right to form tenant cooperatives owning and running their management and budget for themselves. They will also have the right to ask other institutions to take over their housing. We will give each council house tenant individually the right to transfer the ownership of his or her house to a housing association or other independent approved landlord.[52]

A series of amendments both preceding and following this declaration gave force to it. The Housing Act of 1985[53] provided that a tenants' association with 50% membership may apply to local authorities to acquire or manage a building or project and must be given an answer within six months. The Housing Act of 1988 provides for a ballot of tenants about the establishment of Housing Action Trusts, to replace existing management.[54] The Local Government and Housing Act of 1989 provided that where tenants in an Urban Renewal Area are obliged under leases to repair common areas, three fourths of them may apply for a repair grant.[55] Another provision applicable to terrace housing provides for group repairs schemes on application of 75% of owners in the group.[56]

A provision of the Landlord and Tenant Act of 1985[57] provided for certification of tenants' associations by members of local rent assessment committees and, as amended in 1987, gave associations thus certified the right to be consulted concerning employment of management agents and the right to propose contractors. Earlier, the Housing and Building Control Act of 1984 gave tenants the right to make repairs, and the Housing Act of 1962 had facilitated the formation of Housing Associations to build houses, while the Housing Act of 1975 provided for the creation of Housing Management Cooperatives. These acts in combination permitted contiguous homeowners to establish Development Trusts to both improve and maintain contiguous houses, leading architects promoting these schemes to observe "[T]he idea of the Community, even a small section of it, as its own developer, takes some getting used to."[58] The Birmingham Housing Authority adopted a program involving minor improvements such as roof repairs, window painting, and uniform railings for each house on a street. The cause of tenant management has also been embraced by the Labour-dominated Association of London Authorities.[59]

TRAFFIC CALMING

Two other forms of cooperation among neighbors arise from recent legislation. A series of enactments, most of them contemplating consent or consultation of neighbors, permit the creation of play streets or dual-use streets, or the use of traffic calming devices. The earliest such enactment was the Manchester Corporation Act of 1934[60] authorizing play streets. Following the issuance by the Ministry of Transport of Colin Buchanan's *Traffic in Towns* in 1963,[61] the Highways Act of 1980[62] authorized the use of varying street widths, and the Local Government (Miscellaneous Provisions) Act of 1982[63] authorized the placement of structures on walkways and highways with the consent of occupiers of buildings as to walkways and with the consent of owners and occupiers as to highways "for the purpose of giving effect to a pedestrian planning order, [or] enhancing the amenity of the highway, [or] providing a service for the benefit of the public." Finally, the Traffic Calming Act of 1992 authorized traffic calming works and provided for promulgation of requirements "as to consultation and publicity in respect of proposed works." Existing street-closing legislation, more cumbersome than its Continental equivalents, requires "publication of a notice, a 21-day objection period, approval by the local planning commission, and submission to the Secretary of State," a national official.[64] These measures in combination bid fair to result in at least informal street associations. "In the Netherlands [and in Bologna], the particular traffic-control devices are left for residents of the streets to determine through a sophisticated process of citizen participation."[65]

LEASEHOLD ENFRANCHISEMENT

A second legal change with more dubious effects on community was brought about by enactment of the Leasehold Reform Housing and Urban Development Act of 1993, providing for enfranchisement of leaseholders, principally those in the City of London paying ground rent to landowners such as the Duke of Westminster. Of this system Lewis Mumford wrote:

Feudal land was leased for 99 or 999 years. This system favored continuity and it slowed the upward movement of prices. . . . The more dense the occupation, the higher the income; the higher the income, the higher the capitalizable value of the land. Cities like London for long escaped the worst results of this vicious cycle through the fact that much of the land was in feudalholdings or long-term leases.[66]

A more recent commentator, Anthony Sutcliffe, noted:

[T]he leasehold tenure system under which so much of suburban London was developed greatly discouraged purpose-built flats. . . . [L]andlords decided that their site values could best be maintained by low-density, high class housing. The builder . . . did not have to bear the burden of the capital costs of the land and was usually willing to cooperate with the landlord.[67]

The 1993 act impairs this system by allowing two thirds of the tenants occupying one half the flats in a building to exercise a right of enfranchisement to acquire the ground rent.[68] Thereafter, the Minister for Housing may require the landlord to enter into a management agreement with a tenant management organization, and two-thirds of the tenants may require a management audit. Whether this regime will provide for a form of communal government in the previously leased buildings or rather their sale, demolition, and replacement by modern high-rise developments with conventional tenure remains to be seen. "The Leasehold Reform Act raises serious problems for these [aristocratic London] estates, so that the community will be unable to rely on them in the future, as in the past, as the protector of conservation areas."[69]

NEIGHBORHOOD LAW ENFORCEMENT

Finally, the Conservative government has been generous in its support of neighborhood "block watch" schemes,[70] generally organized by county police rather than at the parish and community level. The Home Secretary recently observed: "There is a chance that public concern could show itself in ways none of us would approve. That makes it ever more important that we channel that concern into constructive action in partnership with the police."[71] More recently, the government has encouraged parish councils to submit schemes for unpaid uniformed constables and parish wardens. [72]

CONDOMINIUMS AND APARTMENT HOUSE COMMUNITIES

The condominium regime, however, has not yet gained a foothold in England. "The problems surrounding the enforcement of positive covenants have severely restricted freehold flat development."[73]

From this survey, it is evident that the principal area for future expansion of "miniature government" in England involves established projects, streets, and buildings in urban areas and the rendition of social services in rural ones. A study comparing the work of voluntary organizations and parish councils concluded that the parish council's advantage lay in continuity and "clear and ready identifiability for the authorities."[74] An earlier study of voluntary work in the welfare state stressed the importance to unwed mothers of play streets and play groups; to schools of organizations such as the London School Care Committee, providing visitors to schools and to the families of schoolchildren, "voluntary recruits to a statutory service"; and to citizens generally of Citizens' Advice Bureaux and Marriage Guidance Councils. It also emphasized the need in new housing estates for "social action . . . to stimulate community feelings"; "much more attention should be paid at the village or district level to

. . . organizational communities, which may range from a very formal association to an informal group of concerned citizens."[75] This conclusion reflects Page Smith's observation that

"[nineteenth-century] American towns were founded by people who themselves held some kind of utopian expectation, while the twentieth-century English communities have been planned by people who wished to create utopias for others. . . . [T]he American town builders saw utopia as being achieved through the conquest of the human heart, while the British planners have seen it as a triumph of the mind, a victory for "scientific principles."[76]

The architectural determinism of the Garden City movement has in recent years given way to the more balanced approach of Octavia Hill, a housing reformer as well as historic preservationist once stigmatized as paternalistic and retrograde:

[It is] not so much a question of dealing with houses alone, as of dealing with houses in connection with their influence on the character and habits of people who inhabit them.
. . . [y]ou cannot deal with the people and their houses separately . . . transplant them tomorrow to healthy and commodious houses and they would pollute and destroy them.[77]

The need for the social organization of new housing estates was the subject of a report published by the Council House Communities in 1980[78] and a report of the Audit Commission in 1986,[79] the first stressing the importance of community meeting places, the second emphasized the importance of "defensible" space[80] measures to reduce the perceived scale and anonymity of projects and the creation of tenants' associations[81] to welcome new tenants, identify low-cost improvements, ensure that communal facilities are maintained, and encourage a sense of joint ownership.

The need for community meeting places and for Social Relations officers in new housing estates had been recognized at least as early as 1965: "[T]o build houses without parallel provision of community facilities and amenities will result in the unnecessary creation of social problems. . . . What is saved and more may have to be spent by the personal social services in the rescue of families in distress."[82]

Even earlier, in 1962, another study of new housing estates concluded that a public body other than a tenants' association was needed, since such associations frequently developed adversarial relationships with the authorities.

"Children's playgrounds, the provision of telephones and local post offices or even stamp machines, road intersections, grass verges or the fencing of gardens, the provision of garages and conveniently placed shops loom large in the local picture. . . . It is by starting with the small and concrete that some idea of the objects, methods and limits of local government can most easily be imparted . . . [i]t appears illogical that the corporate rights insured to smaller rural populations should be entirely lacking in the large towns."[83]

Proposed architectural devices included restriction of walkways from above ground level, fencing of each building, limiting gaps in perimeter walls to one, inclusion of gates and gateposts, walling off of services from residences, limiting access to one staircase, limiting the number of dwellings on each entry, providing for ground floor flats near entrances, and ensuring that entrances have glazed doors and are visible from streets.

British policy in this sphere has come a long way since a Minister of Housing's infamous memorandum of 25 years ago: "[t]he PM has committed us to industrialized building and I see nothing to lose if we make the local authorities turn over to it, since conventional architecture is so terrible it couldn't be worse."[84]

HISTORIC PRESERVATION

In England, as in the United States, local desires for special planning regimes have given rise to the creation of historic preservation districts, though the designation is by the national government without the element of formal submunicipal participation present in the United States and France. As of 1992, there were 6,300 designated conservation areas in England and Wales.[85] One commentator inquires "Do not areas of poorer environmental quality need [designation] even more?"[86]

CONCLUSION

The developments here recounted would at least have pleased Arnold Toynbee, who in one of his valedictory works observed:

These present-day ex-rural deracines have been dumped in a warren of streets and houses in which they are physically at close quarters but are spiritually still far apart from each other. Their crying need is to be given a chance to strike fresh roots in their new unfamiliar and excruciating environment and to become each others' neighbors there in the social as well as the physical sense. The most promising social strategy for meeting that need is to try to articulate each of the megalopolises of today . . . into cells on the city-state scale and with the city-state standard of sociability. . . . In an urban community on the village scale the waif, marooned in the world-city's "lonely crowd," will have a chance of becoming once more a member of a community, and this is a human waif's birthright, since man is by nature a social being.   In virtue of its performance of this social function, the village-size component of the world-city will be the most important one of all.[87]

NOTES

1. A. Mabileau et al., *Local Politics and Participation in Britain and France* (1989), at 3.

2. A. de Tocqueville, *Democracy in America* (Vintage ed.), at 924.

3. P. Quentin, *In Search of Community Spirit*, in Mabileau et al., *supra*, note 1 at 237.

4. S. Webb and B. Webb, *The Development of English Local Government* (1963 ed.), at 9.

5. 2 & 3 Philip and Mary ch. 8 (1555).

6. S. Webb and B. Webb, 1 *English Local Government: The Story of the King's Highway* (1920), at 29. In France, an obligation of three days' service repairing local roads continued to be owed to communes and survived until at least 1911, though in 1903 a law was passed allowing the communes to convert the tax in kind to a money tax, the hiring of substitutes having long been allowed. T. Zeldin, 1 *France 1848-1945* (1983).

7. Webb and Webb, *supra* note 4, at 9.

8. *Id.* at 38.

9. 5 Eliz. c. 3 (1563); see *id.* at 51.

10. 9 George I. c. 7 (1723).

11. Webb and Webb, *supra* note 4, at 6.

12. S. Webb and B. Webb, 7 *English Local Government: The Old Poor Law* (1927), at 298.

13. *Id.* at 321.

14. *Id.* at 427.

15. J. Redlich and Hirst, 2 *Local Government in England* (1903), at 204-5.

16. 1 S. Webb and B. Webb, 1 *English Local Government: The Parish and the County* (1906), at 172.

17. 1 Edw. I. stat. 2 (1285).

18. Hay & Snyder, *infra* note 19 at 56.

19. See generally P. Pringle: *Hue and Cry* (1969), D. Hay and Snyder, *Policing and Prosecution in England, 1750-1850* (1988), at 56, 94-95. On the Local Government Act of 1858, see J. Prest, *Liberty and Locality: Parliament, Permissive Legislation and Ratepayer' Democracies in the Nineteenth Century* (1990), at 218.

20. Redlich and Hirst, *supra* note 15, at 170, quoting a speech of Sir Henry Fowler (Hansard, 21 March 1893).

21. 57 & 58 Vict. ch. 73.

22. V. Lipman, *Local Government Areas 1834-1945* (1949), at 151.

23. *Parliamentary Debates*, Third Series, 324 at cols. 1804-9.

24. Lipman, *supra* note 22, at 159, citing R. Ensor, *The Supersession of County Government*, Politica (1935), at 425; G. Brodrick, *Local Government in England, in Local Government and Local Taxation* (1882).

25. Redlich and Hirst, *supra* note 15, at 183.

26. Local Government Act of 1894, sec. 6(1).

27. Redlich and Hirst, *supra* note 15 at 192; Local Government Act of 1894, sec. 8(3).

28. Local Government Act of 1894, secs. 13(2), 26(4).

29. *Id.*, sec. 8(2).

30. Redlich and Hirst, *supra* note 15, at 197.

31. The quotation relating to the education reforms is from A. Wright, *Citizens and Subjects: An Essay on British Politics* (1994), at 108. Also see *Written Evidence . . . to the Royal Commission or Local Government in England*, (1969) at 162, par. 3.

32. *Written Evidence, supra* note 31, par. 4.

33. *Id.* at 164, par. 9.

34. Mabileau et al., *supra* note 1, at 33.

35. *Written Evidence, supra* note 31, at 165, par. 13.

36. *Id.* at 165, par. 14. See Department of the Environment, *Roles and Activities of Parish and Town Councils in England: Case Studies* (1993), at par. 9.1.

37. *Id.* at 167, par. 23.

38. *Id.* at 167, par. 24.

39. *Id.* at 168, par. 27.

40. Royal Commission on Local Government in England, 1 Report (Cmnd. 4040)(1969), at 382. An advisory group on neighborhood councils declared in 1977: "Statutory provision should have been made for neighborhood councils when we went through the trauma of reorganization of local government. Such provision was made in Scotland and--to some extent--for Wales." From Department of the Environment, *The Neighborhood Council* (1977).

41. On Evelyn Sharp, see E. Sharp, *Parish Pump in the 70's*, Manchester Guardian 10 (19 December 1969).

42. Missing citation to quote from Royal Commission

43. 335 *Hansard (Lords),* (18 September 1972), at cols. 814-26. See also Department of the Environment, *The Future of Parishes and Neighborhoods* (1971). See S. Hatch, ed., *Toward Participation in Local Services* (1973), at 50; Scottish Development Department, *Community Councils* (1974); C. Clarke, *Community Councils: Power to the People*, in 3 *Participation in Politics: British Political Sociology Yearbook*, (C. Crouch ed. 1977), at 110-42.

44. Department of the Environment, *The Future of Parishes and Neighborhoods* (1971).

45. G. Daniel, Participation in Community Life, opening address to the Seventh British Conference on Social Welfare, April 1970, quoted in I. Rees, *Government by Community* (1971), 84-85. See also Department of the Environment, *supra* note 36, at E. 54.

46. M. Bulmer ed., *Neighbors: The Work of Philip Abrams* (1986).

47. See P. Abrams, *Neighborhood Care and Social Policy* (1989); Ministry of Health, *The Development of Community Care* (1973); *Report of the Committee on Local Authority and Allied Services (Seebohn Report)* (1968); Department of Health and Social Security, *A Happier Old Age* (1977); Department of Health and Social Security, *Care in the Community* (1983); House of Commons, *Community Care* (1985); Audit Commission, *Making Community Care a Reality* (1986); National Audit Office, *Community Care Developments* (1987); Department of Health and Social Security, *Community Care: Agenda for Action* (1988); House of Commons, *Community Care Developments* (1988); Department of Health and Social Security, *Caring for People* (Cm. 849) (1989).

The Conservative government has not embraced the proposition that there is a need for the "development of secondary structures for the fostering of local attachment. Such mediating structures are not 'natural'; they have to be created." M. Bulmer, *The Social Basis of Community Care* (1987); see Home Office, *Community Work and the Probation Service* (1991).

48. Welsh Department, *Local Government in Wales: A Charter for the Future* (Cm. 2155) (March 1993), at secs. 7.2, 7.7.

49. Scottish Department, *The Structure of Scottish Local Government: Shaping the Future: The New Councils*, (Cm. 2267) (July 1993), at Sec. 6.5. A 1975 report had urged that "responsibilities which could be transferred (along with suitable resources) from local authorities to community associations include the management of community and recreation facilities and the undertaking of a measure of preventive social work, for instance the support of disadvantaged individuals or groups within the community." From the Scottish Department, *Report of Morris Committee on Links Between Housing and Social Work* (1975), at par. 9.24. For similar organizations in Edmonton, Alberta, see J. Slack, *Community Leagues: A Canadian Concept for the Delivery of Municipal Services*, 10 Local Government Studies (N.S.) 21 (1984). The quotation from the Webbs is at S. Webb and B. Webb, *A Constitution for the Socialist Commonwealth of Great Britain* (3d ed. 1975), at 223, 225.

50. On the Local Government Commission, see K. Poole, *100 and Not Out Yet*, Local Government Chronicle, 17 December 1993, at 18.

51. The quotation from the Webbs is at S. Webb and B. Webb, *A Constitution for the Socialist Commonwealth of Great Britain* (3d ed. 1975), at 223, 225.

52. Conservative Party, *Manifesto* (1987).

53. Housing Act of 1985, ch. 68, sec. 27C.

54. Housing Act of 1988, ch. 93, sec. 61(3).

55. Local Government and Housing Act of 1989, ch. 42, secs. 105(2)(c), 111. See A. Power, *Local Housing Management: A Priority Estates Project* (1989).

56. Local Government and Housing Act of 1989, ch. 42, sec. 127.

57. Landlord and Tenant Act of 1985, secs. 19, 29, 30B; Landlord and Tenant Act of 1987, sec. 41(1), sch. 2, par. 3.

58. See T. Gibson, *Counterweight: The Neighborhood Option* (1984), at 55, 56, 96, 222-24; D. Rock, *Grassroots Developers* (1986).

59. Association of London Authorities, *Tenants in Power: A Radical Alternative to the Government's Public Housing Proposals* (1988).

60. 1934 Local Acts, ch. 97, secs. 43-45.

61. C. Buchanan, *Traffic in Towns* (1963).

62. Highways Act of 1980, ch. 66, sec 75.

63. Local Government (Miscellaneous Provisions) Act of 1982, s. 20, sch. 5. pt. 1. par. 1.

64. Traffic Calming Act of 1992, ch. 30, enacting Highways Act of 1980, secs. 90 G-I. See C. Hass-Klau, *Environmental Traffic Management In Britain: Does It Exist?* 12 Built Environment 7 (1986); and on pre-existing procedure, see R. Brambilla et al., *For Pedestrians Only* (1977), at 65, which also discusses Bologna.

65. N. Pressman, *The European Experience,* in *Public Streets for Public Use* (A. Moudon ed. 1987), 40, 42.

66. L. Mumford, *The Culture of Cities* (1961), at 418.

67. A. Sutcliffe, *Multi-Story Living* (1974), at 12.

68. Leasehold Reform, Housing and Urban Development Act of 1993, ch. 28. Lessors of individual homes had been accorded a right of purchase since the Leasehold Reform Act of 1967, so that the legislation did not represent an innovation in principle. N. Hague, *Leasehold Enfranchisement* (2d ed. 1987).

69. On effects of the act, see Royal Institute of Chartered Surveyors, *Report*, in *Conservation and Development in Historic Towns and Cities* (P. Ward ed. 1968), at 13, 19-20.

70. See T. Hope and M. Shaw, *Communities and Crime Reduction* (1990); T. Bennett, *Evaluating Neighborhood Watch* (1990); P. Wilson, *Trends and Issues in Crime and Criminal Justice* (1990).

71. London Times, 13 October 1992, at 2. These observations have been carried further:

If it is true, as the police in London informally admit, that they have a policy of not investigating most crime, why should citizens not be able to form their own "vigilante" groups, with a police liaison allowing them to use computer and other records? The rule of law as it becomes weaker, has also become more statist. . . . [The police] accumulate more powers and privileges and operate a closed shop. From London Sunday Telegraph, 17 October 1993, at 25.

72. On parish constables and parish wardens, see C. Aslet, *Specials to their Manor Born*, Independent, 11 October 1993, at 19; London Times, 20 July 1993, at 22; *idem*, 3 September 1993, at 8.

73. Law Commission, *Report on Law of Positive and Restrictive Covenants*, (Report 127) (1989); Wilberforce Commission, *Report on Positive Covenants Affecting Land*, (Cmnd. 2719) (1965).

74. P. Stringer, *A Comparison of Parish Councils and Voluntary Organizations in Action*, 10 Journal of Voluntary Action Research 62 (1981).

75. M. Morris, *Voluntary Work in the Welfare State* (1969), at 24, 31, 101, 175, 180. See Bulmer, *supra* note 47, at 208-9.

76. P. Smith, *As a City Upon a Hill: The Town in American History* (1968), at 29.

77. E.M. Bell, *Octavia Hill*, (1942).

78. Council House Communities, *Report by a Subcommittee of the Scottish Housing Advisory Committee* (1970). Of Octavia Hill, it has been said: [Her] idea was really a very simple one: merely that competent disinterested people should take over the management of tenement buildings on behalf of the owners and that, through keeping them on a strictly paying basis, they should by example and education gradually introduce a modicum of cooperative order and cleanliness and decency." From C.Bauer, *Modern Housing* (1935), at 86.

79. Audit Commission, *Managing the Crisis in Council Housing* (1986), at 21, 37.

80. O. Newman, *Communities of Interest* (1972).

81. T. Aldous, *Urban Villages* (1992), at 89-92. The most influential British work on "defensible space" is A. Coleman, *Utopia on Trial* (1988). Compare B. Hiller, *City of Alice's Dreams*, Architects' Journal, 9 July 1986, at 39-41; see also Department of the Environment, *Crime Prevention on Council Estates* (1993), urging that design changes be accompanied by local management initiatives, security measures, social measures for young people, and changes in police arrangements.

82. Ministry of Housing and Local Government, *The Needs of New Communities* (1967), at par. 330.

83. H. Jennings, *Societies in the Making* (1962), at 238, 239.

84. R. Crossman, *Diaries of a Cabinet Minister* (1975), at 131.

85. See Civic Amenities Act of 1967; Planning (Listed Buildings and Conservation Areas) Act of 1990, sec. 9; J. Delafons, *The Conservation See-Saw*, 62 Town and Country Planning 227 (1993).

86. S. Payne, *Too Conservative a Solution: The Conservation Area Test*, 55 Modern Law Review 726 (1992).

87. A. Toynbee, *Cities on the Move* (1970), at 64, 245.

2

France—The Catholic, Radical, and Anarchist Commune

French villages and towns possess much greater political and financial powers than their British counterparts. The powers of the thousands of traditional communes are more than historical remnants and have recently been enhanced by relief from prefectural supervision and by increased revenue and tax sharing. They extend to such matters as planning permission, the construction of elementary schools, and water and sewer services. However, communal powers tend to be concentrated in the mayor, who frequently also serves at other layers of government; councils do not have the importance they do in Britain.

French city dwellers likewise possess political institutions of greater significance than their British counterparts. The small cities are divided into their historic communes--the three largest into arrondissements, which provide sub-municipal councils to neighborhoods of about 50,000 people, although these entities have only limited budgets and powers and no power of taxation.

The intellectual and political history of France can be traced through the waning and waxing of the powers of the traditional unit of French local government, the commune. Although since the Revolution France is popularly thought of as the epitome of the centralized state, the commune, an entity with feudal origins, has been sustained not only by traditionalist conservatism but by anarchist and Catholic strains in French thinking.

HISTORY OF THE COMMUNE

In point of theory, the commune, an extraordinarily small entity frequently resembling in size the American residential community association, is the basis of local government in France. It constituted a secularized version of the former parish, and many existing communes can trace their history for 900 years. There are approximately 36,000 communes, or 1 for every 1,500 Frenchmen, disposing of 27.1% of public expenditure.[1]

Although the durability of the commune is impressive, its independence and functions have fluctuated over time. The Revolution in 1790 provided it with elected assemblies, which were expressly subordinate to the National Assembly. In 1799, under Napoleon, communal mayors were made appointees of the central government and subordinated to prefects, a "name itself borrowed from imperial Rome, reflect[ing] the cult of Rome fashionable during and after the Revolution."[2] Although central control was somewhat relaxed by measures in 1831, 1867, and 1871, it was not until 1887 that mayors were again subject to election by town councils. They have remained so, save during the Vichy period.[3]

The historic functions of the communes included the maintenance of purely local amenities; the management of communal property; the letting of contracts for sewers, roads, and other local improvements; and the local discharge of various central government functions. In fact, the independence of the communes was severely qualified. Because the role of communal councils was limited to approval of the budget, which in turn was subject to approval by a centrally appointed prefect, the vigor and independence of the commune were in no small measure a function of the personality of the mayor, whose powers were frequently supplemented by the holding of departmental, regional, or natural office under the practice known as *cumule des mandats*: "The Radical party, with its reliance on local notables and weak party discipline was . . . superbly adapted to the Third and Fourth Republics."[4]

As of 1981, the communes collectively had 725,000 employees, as against 2.6 million employees of the central government, a ratio almost the exact reverse of that in England. Yet in part by reason of the fact that there are nearly a half million mayors and municipal counselors in France, a study in 1989 concluded: "The findings [as to] the actual extent of democratic participation . . . often run counter to what one might have expected. Although only a low level of local democratic activity is to be found in either country, it appears higher in France."[5]

The general tendency since the war has been in the direction of at least formal decentralization of the rigidly centralized Jacobin system. Article 87 of the 1946 Constitution misleadingly declared, given the persistence of prefectorial supervision, "local authorities will be self-administering with councils elected by universal suffrage. Their decisions will be put into practice under the supervision of the Mayor."

While the 1887 law in theory gave communes the right to "provide any service which they deem necessary or useful for the welfare of the community,"[6] the exercise of this power was subject to central government supervision, as well as supervision by the Council d'Etat, which could decide whether a service is "genuinely in the local interest."

A law of 1890 permitted joint action among communes. In 1958, joint action was made compulsory when two thirds of the councils representing half the population or half the councils representing two thirds of the population in any of 288 agglomerations requested such joint action. The powers of communes with respect to schools were limited to the construction (but not staff and curriculum) of grammar schools. Since 1941, towns over 10,000 have had no responsibility for appointment or dismissal of policemen; smaller communities appoint their own constables. Public welfare claims are still made to the commune in the first instance, though the role of the department in administering claims was greatly increased in 1956.

URBAN SUBDIVISIONS

Many large cities are divided into small historic communes, the major exceptions being Paris, Lyons, and Marseilles, which are divided into arrondisements, 20 in the case of Paris, with relatively minor powers involving vital statistics registration. In 1966, "urban communities" were established for other major cities, the existing communes within them retaining relatively minor operational powers together with the power to elect the council of the urban community.[7]

RECENT REFORMS

In March 1968, this movement toward centralization was abruptly checked by a famous speech at Lyon by General Charles de Gaulle, which made decentralization a burning issue in France for the next 15 years. In it, the president declared:

The centuries-old centralizing effort required to achieve and sustain [France's] unity is no longer necessary. On the contrary, it is regional development that will provide the motive force of its future economic power.[8]

De Gaulle had long been troubled by the extent of France's centralization. In a passage on American government buried in his discussion of the 1946 constitution in his memoirs,[9] he observed:

Other[s] . . . advocated the so-called "presidential system" on the American pattern . . . Executive and legislative would thus go through the whole duration of their respective mandates without either of them ever being able to coerce the other . . . [The United States] is a federation of states each of which, with its governor, its representatives, its judges, and its officials--all elected--takes upon itself responsibility for a large part of the immediate business of politics, administration, justice, public order, economy, health, education, etc. while the central government and Congress normally confine themselves to larger matters; foreign policy, civic rights and duties, defense, currency, overall taxes and tariffs. For these reasons where would it lead France . . . a country the demands of whose unity coupled with the perpetual threats from outside have induced to centralize its administration to the utmost, thus making it ipso facto the target of every grievance? . . . The inevitable result would be either the submission of the President to the demands of the deputies or else a pronunciamento.[10]

The proposals brought forward by de Gaulle after the May 1968 crisis were rejected by 53% of the electors in a referendum, less on their merits than as a result of their association with de Gaulle. An additional factor leading to rejection was the opposition of communal notables to reconstruction of the French Senate, which would have reduced it to a consultative role and added appointed representatives of professional groups to the existing membership chosen by municipal counselors, the Senate traditionally having been referred to as a *grand conseil des communes de France*.[11]

Following the referendum, limited reforms were carried out by the Pompidou government in 1970-72.[12] Pompidou feared regional government. "What we must encourage are the little and middle-sized towns where the quality of life is good . . . Let us industrialize within the framework of the structure which grew out of our history and geography."[13] By a law of 31 December, 1970, municipal budgets no longer required advance approval of prefects and were permitted to take effect if not vetoed within 15 days; mayors were permitted to delegate powers to assistants; and state subsidies to municipalities could be awarded by regional officials without reference to Paris. In 1971, an effort known as the Marcellin Law was made to force the grouping of communes. Although very few communes surrendered their separate existence, by 1983, 3,000 syndicates of communes managed by boards on which each member commune is represented had been established, embracing about half of all communes and about half the French population.[14] The Marcellin Law granted consolidating communes a 50% increase in certain subsidies. In 1972, regional councils were established, half of whose members were elected by general and municipal counselors. The emphasis on large regions was described as a form of "disguised centralization."[15]

The ensuing Giscard government appointed a study commission that reported in 1976 but whose proposals were vitiated by opposition in the municipally controlled Senate. In Giscard's view, the commune was "too involved with itself" to coordinate economic development, though it remained "the site of local democracy, the organ of decentralized, elected power, the institution through which Frenchmen and Frenchwomen can take charge of their daily lives, provided they are given the responsibilities and the means to carry them out."[16]

The advent of the Mitterand government had been preceded by a "march through the institutions" arising from Socialist control of various local governments and by important new influences on the Socialists. Disillusionment with nationalized structures manifested itself in the May 1968 disturbances, and Khrushchev's exposure of Stalinist abuses had a greater reverberation in Paris than elsewhere, giving rise to a "new left" of autogestionnaires interested in decentralization of at least the workplace. The collapse of the Catholic MRP party as a result of the Indochina and Algerian wars drove at least some Catholic intellectuals to the Left.

The Catholic view of society has always been more corporate than the secular republican one; it respects intermediate associations, both public and private. Its criticism of capitalism applies also to the French version of democracy; the individual is atomized by market forces in the economy and politics. Unions, associations, local governments, regions--these all help root the individual in a series of meaningful relationships in which the development of personality and the exercise of freedom can occur."[17]

In Grenoble, a Socialist mayor created advisory community councils in six town quarters; in other cities, councils provided for solar energy developments, increases in social security payments, and pedestrianization of town centers. The Socialists contemplated "a role for local government in building up the small and medium sized business sector."[18] Of course, strengthening community government had its dangers, notably that of "local totalitarianism with more pressure on nonconforming individuals than might be found in a larger grouping. To combat this, the socialists would institute proportional representation and encourage the growth of associations and the institutions of civil society."[19] The Socialist party was not trade-union based, unlike the Labor party in England, the Social Democrats in Germany and to a large degree, the Democratic party in the United States and had an "ability to accommodate pluralist, decentralist and autogestionnaire ideas often shunned by the solidaristic and centralist tendencies of trade-union based parties."[20]

An act of March 1982 on the Rights and Liberties of Communes abolished the veto of the prefect over communal laws. Notification of the prefect is still required, and he may refer new laws to the Conseil d'etat for a determination of their validity. Financial controls were relaxed by use of a new postaudit system,[21] from which communes with populations of 2,000 or less were exempted in 1986.

A 1983 law provided for a form of proportional representation in municipal councils.

Now opposition representatives will have a continuing political platform and by pursuing local issues and complaints, the means to build a political base. This could be particularly true of the poorer quarters of those cities traditionally controlled by the right."[22]

A proposal to alter municipal governments in Paris, Lyon, and Marseilles was enacted in altered form to enhance the powers of Parisian arrondisements and those of Marseilles and Lyon. The arrondisement councils were given advisory power over planning applications, the power to carry out state functions relating to vital statistics, and powers to look after "creches, youth facilities, gymnasiums, gardens and open spaces and old people's homes."[23] Each arrondisement was accorded approximately 40 civil servants; the 1984 budget for all 20 Paris subdivisions was about Fr300 million, or about $2 million per arrondisement. The supporters of Mayor Chirac gained control of all 20 local councils at the 1982 elections, causing the system to get off to a slow start. A skeptic has complained that mayor and people are now separated by "a screen composed firstly of well-educated self-appointed demagogues in each quartier--and secondly--paid social workers and animators who construe self-management as management by themselves, the professionals."[24]

In 1983, additional legislation gave communes the right to grant building permits pursuant to commune-proposed plans that are subject to national review. Mayors not wishing this power may relinquish it to the national government after each election.[25] As of January 1986, 80% of communes with more than 2000 persons had adopted plans, and 36% of smaller communes had done so. "Procedures have been simplified to encourage many more small communes to prepare them, and the state has provided more funds to finance their preparation."[26] On the other hand, one observer contends that "the lack of suitable personnel and the inadequate funding at the communal level, compounded by the complexities of the legislation itself, have left the state in still a controlling position. *Plus ca change--plus c'est la meme chose!*"[27]

A major local victory contained in the loi Deferre was an ambiguous clause permitting localities to engage in economic activities. No one really knows what this means, but neither are central officials snuffing out local economic experiments. Several more progressive towns in the Isere . . . are joint partners in buyouts and industrial ventures to create jobs. The centrist mayor of one large city, Nimes, used his new powers to create a communal minimum income."[28]

Communes also were confirmed in their responsibility for constructing and maintaining elementary schools and were given new power to regulate holidays and the after-school use of school buildings. In 1980, communes were also given the right to change the balance among the four principal local taxes on property and payrolls, rather than requesting proportionate changes in them. In 1979, the

Giscard government had given the communes a formula grant for investment and services limited to the notional yield of the value-added tax, thus lessening reliance on project grants. Other formula grants reward actual investment by communes.

In addition, an abortive effort was made to give communes a role in educational policy by allowing them to approve or disapprove assistance to private primary schools. This proposal was invalidated by a decision dated 18 January 1985, of the French Constitutional Court, which reasoned in somewhat Jacobin fashion that

even if the principle of the free administration of local authorities has constitutional value, it should not lead to the result that essential conditions for the implementation of a loi organizing the exercise of a civil liberty should depend on decisions of local authorities and thus might not be the same throughout the country."[29]

A further change, with centralizing potential, establishes a new corps of local administrators, who may elect to work in central government.

Evaluation of the effect of the Mitterand reforms would be premature. The fiscal stringency and deregulatory tendency of the 1980s worked against a dramatic growth in the self-confidence with which new local powers were exercised, since "the liberal vision focusses on the freedom of the individual and the firm, not that of the collectivity."[30] Two students of the changes have concluded that "The commune, despite the existence of many tiny communes whose functional viability is very much in doubt, retains a vitality as the expression of a localist democracy which has disappeared in many other parts of Europe."[31] A study of the reforms in 1990 concluded that they "[b]roke up the system of complicity with the prefect" and that the new system reduced from two months to three weeks the time necessary to issue a building permit. Further, the decentralization measures gave communes significant flexibility to adjust their priorities in periods of austerity. Although the communes realized only 2% of the revenues transferred to subnational governments from the decentralization reforms, the adoption of formula grants, the abolition of the *tutelle*, and the provision of new taxing authorities have benefited them. Since 1980, communes decide their own rate of taxation, and 35% of their revenues are from their own local taxes. In addition, "since 1987, municipalities have been allowed more freedom in establishing fees and costs of local public services, the increase of which was previously severely restricted by central government."[32]

FEDERATED COMMUNES

In 1990 and 1991, a number of measures of an equalizing nature were imposed on the communes. The Housing Act of 1990 allowed prefects to impose some social housing on reluctant communes. A system known as the Dotations Sociales Urbaines of May 1991 provides for transfer of some taxing resources from richer to poorer communes and provides for sharing of the professional tax by communes throughout an urban area.

It would clearly be a mistake to too early denigrate the viability of the very small communes. Even small communes can render services, as do many American residential community associations, by contracting out to private companies such matters as garbage collection and water supply. This has led one writer to note that

the French system is one of "local government" and not of local agencies. . . . The municipalities are independent and small in size . . . but the system works because the large multisector companies reintroduce scale economics . . . political legitimacy is above technical legitimacy; political control restrains professionalism"[33]

HOUSING COMMUNITIES

In addition to the commune and arrondisement, several other forms of community government have emerged in France. Early efforts to build blocks of workers' housing around central courtyards were resisted on the premise that the "grouping of large numbers of workers together [was] socially undesirable [because of] the link between socialist thought and community housing projects."[34]

Early workers' projects were characterized by

controls . . . such as the shutting of the main gates at night, or the discouragement of gathering in groups. The reformers used the understandable objection to such regulation as evidence that workers themselves disliked dense blocks of flats, but the very existence of the regulations indicated that the reaction against the blocks steamed initially from those who did not have to live in them, rather than those who did.[35]

Instead, workers' flats took the form of "flats grouped around staircases, with direct access to each stair from the street."[36] To this was ultimately added in many places a further measure of social control in the form of the concierge apartment, as to which it was said that the typical Englishman "will not reside in a house in which the staircase is guarded by a man and wife with the chance of an additional incumbrance every ten months and an half."[37]

CONDOMINIUMS

In addition to the concierge apartment, France also was one of the first nations to accept the condominium as an institution. A British lawyer wrote in 1966, quite inaccurately: "[I]f such individualists as the French have contrived to operate co-property with success, it augurs well for its future in England."[38] The French condominium is potentially wider in scope than a single building. As created in 1965, it extends to "any building or group of buildings parts of which are in more than one ownership. . . . [It] can apply also to land owned in common by a number of owners of houses built on that land."[39] The device has been extended to include "[c]o-owned old people's houses, where medical services and transport are provided on a communal basis [by] apportion[ing] the costs of these services without taking into account how much each owner uses the common services."[40]

The French condominium deviates from its American counterpart in a number of respects. "It is common for blocks of flats to have a commercial user on the ground floor."[41] Further, a law of 21 December 1984 expressly permits use of flats as the registered office of new companies for two years after their incorporation. The condominium association is empowered to regulate and allocate parking. One fourth of owners can call meetings. A developer cannot cast more than half the votes at a meeting, irrespective of how many apartments he owns. Supermajority requirements apply to major improvements; unanimity is necessary to remove central heating. The building is to be managed by a syndic, of whom it has been said: "[t]he profession of syndic provided in very many cases a standard of management which would be totally unacceptable in England."[42]

Most French condominiums are in resort areas, lending the same commentator to note that "few flat owners are permanent residents and it is surprising how the standard of management rises when there is a reasonable number of around the year residents." The same commentator takes a jaundiced view of the suitability of the French for the device. "By nature the French are disputatious and upholding of their own rights while evincing less interest in the rights of others. Hence it is inevitable that meetings of flatowners stand to reflect those characteristics rather than adequately deal with management problems."[43] This statement is reminiscent of the equally jaundiced statement of the political philosopher Michael Walzer: "[T]he institutional structures and the mass commitment necessary to sustain civic virtue simply don't exist in contemporary America."[44] Against this may be set the views of Robert Putnam:

"[W]e should expect the creation and destruction of social capital to be marked by virtuous and vicious cycles. . . . Social capital as embodied in horizontal networks of civic engagement bolsters the performance of the polity and the economy rather than the reverse."[45]

HISTORIC PRESERVATION DISTRICTS

The historic preservation districts created by local legislation in the United States and by national designation in Britain exist in France in a form even more privatized than the historic districts in the United States. Although France initially undertook a centralized approach for designation of historic areas by a national agency acting with local advice under the Malraux Act of 1962, dissatisfaction with the displacement of residents in designated areas led to more localized approaches. A statute of 31 December 1976 established local commissions to formulate conservation plans in nationally designated areas. More important, a new mechanism, the Operations Programmes d'Amelioration de l'Habitat, or OPAH, was created, which allows individual owners to unite to make structural repairs to buildings, under agreements with local and national governments. The law simplifies financial procedures and makes available grants from the Fonds d'Amenagement Urbain (FAU), which was set up in 1976 to provide money "for the improvement of existing urban areas and especially the quality of life and living conditions of property owners with limited means."[46]

The typical OPAH includes 300 buildings or less, and there is a three-year time limit for completing work. Studies must include a "social budget" to predict the impact of rehabilitation on the local population. The plans are frequently accompanied by creation of additional open space and the pedestrianization of streets.[47]

While the nationally protected areas under the Malraux Act numbered 61 after 20 years, no fewer than 379 OPAHs had been instituted in the first 3 years of the scheme. OPAHs like the American historic districts need not involve distinguished architecture where buildings are "united by age, scale, and general harmony."[48]

APARTMENT PROJECTS

Finally, France has had to deal with the problems of large suburban high-rise housing projects; the so-called *grand ensembles*. De Gaulle's abortive regionalization proposals of 1968 called for "A new legal entity, the *ensemble urbain*, [to be] created where at least 7500 new housing units are planned and the population is to increase tenfold. Administration will be in the hands of appointed committees until 40 percent of the new residents are established."[49] This project was realized with construction of nine *villes nouvelles*, which are required to seek approval from the syndicates of the communes in their areas. The state agency regulates construction in the new zone; the communes maintain authority over existing structures.

In due course it was found that "grands ensembles have come to house a disproportionate number of disadvantaged people, whose living conditions are depressed further by unsatisfactory housing and inadequate services and amenities."[50] They differed from the British New Towns in that they were built much closer to existing cities, their blocks were much higher-rise, and their planning was far less coherent. The high-rise *grands ensembles* concept was abandoned in 1972. A report by a Special Commission, the Commission National pour le Development Social des Quartiers, in 1985 concluded that

improvement of the social environment was as important as the more traditional approach of seeking a solution essentially through the refurbishment of property. . . . Some form of local decision-making structure was considered essential, given the complex and comprehensive nature of the proposed rehabilitation and the variations in conditions which existed between sites . . . The active participation of residents in the design of improvements represented a further priority.[51]

NOTES

1. R. Baxley and G. Stoker, *Local Government in Europe: Trends and Developments* (1991), at 105.

2. F. Ridley and J. Blondel, *Public Administration in France* (2d ed. 1969), at 85.

3. D. Bien and R. Grew, *France*, in *Crises of Political Development in Europe and the United States* (R. Grew ed. 1978), at 253; see also, T. Zeldin, *France 1848-1945* (1983), at 527-28.

4. Bien and Grew, *supra* note 3.

5. A. Mabileau et al, *Local Politics and Participation in Britain and France* (1989), at 240. See also Pugsley, *French Local Authority Meetings*, 18 Local Government Review, September 1982; S. Garrish, *Centralization and Decentralization in England and France* (1986); I. Wilson, *Decentralizing or Recentralizing the State*, in *Socialism, the State, and Public Policy* (P. Cerny ed. 1985); P. Booth, *Decision Making and Decentralization: Development Control in France* (1985).

6. Ridley and Blondel, *supra* note 2, at 100.

7. *Id.* at 352.

8. Quoted in M. Keating and P. Hainsworth, *Decentralization and Change in Contemporary France* (1986), at 26.

9. De Gaulle, *Memoirs of Hope: Renewal and Endeavor* (1971), at 323-24.

10. A. Peyrefitte, *LeMal Francais* (1976), at 455, quoted in Gourevitch, *infra* note 17, at 138.

11. Keating and Hainsworth, *supra* note 8, at 27.

12. *Id.* at 28.

13. *Id.*

14. J. Punter, *Planning Control in France*, 59 Town Planning Review 159, 162 (1988).

15. V. Wright and H. Machin, *The French Regional Reform of July 1972: A Case of Disguised Centralization*, 3 Policy and Politics 3-28 (1975). See also R. Irving, *Regionalism in France*, in *The Failure of the State* (J. Cornford ed. 1975), at 14, 37.

16. Le Monde, 24 November 1975, quoted in Gourevitch, *infra* note 17, at 149.

17. P. Gourevitch, *Paris and the Provinces: The Politics of Local Government Reform in France* (1980), at 161-62.

18. Keating and Hainsworth, *supra* note 8, at 68.

19. *Id.*

20. *Id.*

21. *Id.* at 58.

22. *Id.* at 77. See G. Ross, ed., *The Mitterand Experiment* (1987); A. Levine, *The Transformation of Urban Politics in France*, 29 Urban Affairs Quarterly 383 (1994). See J. Ardagh, *France in the 1980s* (1982), at 317, for the second quotation. On budgets, see W. Safran, *The French Polity* (2d ed. 1985), at 222, 229 n.60.

23. Keating and Hainsworth, *supra* note 8, at 78.

24. J. Ardagh, *France in the 1980's* (1982), at 317.

25. Keating and Hainsworth, *supra* note 8, at 82.

26. J. Punter, *supra* note 14, at 180 (1988).

27. *Id.* at 180. See also on planning, I. Wilson, *The Preparation of Local Plans in France*, 54 Town Planning Review (1959), at 172-73; C. Flockton, *French Local Government Reform and Urban Planning*, 9 Local Government Studies (N.S.) 65 (1983).

28. D. Ashford, *British Dogmatism and French Pragmatism Revisited*, in *The New Centralism*, (C. Crouch ed. 1989), at 77, 78.

29. Decision 84-185.

30. Keating and Hainsworth, *supra* note 8, at 130-31.

31. Keating and Hainsworth, *supra* note 8, at 130. See V. Schmidt, *Democratizing France* (1990), 336; 338; V. Hoffman-Matirot, *French Local Policy Change,* in *Urban Innovation and Antonomy* (S. Clarke ed. 1989), at 182-221; P. Le Gales, *New Directions in Decentralizationand Urban Policy in France*, 10 Environment and Planning (1992); V. Schmidt, *Unblocking Politics by Decree*, 22 Comparative Politics 459 (1990).

32. Ashford, *supra* note 28.

33. D. Lorrain, *The French Model for Urban Services*, in *Local Government in Europe: Trends and Developments* (R. Baxley and G. Stoker eds. 1991).

34. N. Bullock and J. Read, *The Movement for Housing Reform in Germany and France 1840-1914* (1985), at 311, 314.

35. *Id.* at 314-15.

36. *Id.* at 317.

37. Tarn, *French Flats for the English*, quoted in A. Sutcliffe, *Multi-Story Living* (1974). A French *grand ensemble* with 1,511 flats, most of them rental properties, included "19 caretakers, all women, [whose] duties are to clean the halls, staircases, and cellars, move the communal dustbins and collect the rents. . . . For these duties they have a rent-free dwelling with heating and lighting and a small wage." From Shankland, Cox and Associates, *La vie dans un grand ensemble* (1971), at sec. 4.8.

38. L. Brown, *French Co-Property of Apartments*, 110 Solicitors Journal 630, 631 (1966). See also J. Hill, *Freehold Flats in French Law*, Conveyancer and Property Lawyer (N.S.) 337 (1985).

39. Act of 10 July 1965; see also Act of 31 December 1985, Statutory Instruments 67-233, 86-768.

40. Hill, *supra* note 38 at 344.

41. H. Dyson, *French Real Property and Succession Law* (2d ed. 1991), at 84.

42. *Id.* at 87.

43. *Id.*

44. M. Walzer, *Radical Principles* (1980), at 67.

45. R. Putnam, *Making Democracy Work: Civic Culture in Italy* (1993), at 170, 175.

46. See R. Kain, *Europe's Model and Exemplar Still? The French Approach to Urban Conservation, 1962-1981*, 53 Town Planning Review 403 (1982); see also F. Sorlin, *The French System for Conservation and Revitalization in Historic Centers*, in *Conservation & Development in Historic Towns and Cities* (P. Ward ed. 1968), at 221-34.

47. *Id.*

48. *Id.*

49. Ridley and Blondel, *supra* at note 2, at 355-56. See B. Ward, *The Process of Local Government Reform, 1966-74* (1976), at 64-65. See also J. Ardagh, *France Today* (1987), at 290-95.

50. Ardagh, *supra* note 49, at 290.

51. I. Tuppen and P. Mingret, *Suburban Malaise in French Cities*, 57 Town Planning Review (1986), at 194-95.

3

Germany—Medieval Localism Revived

German villages retain their traditional *gemeinde* government. Although the *gemeinde* were significantly consolidated in the 1970s, they are still very small units, especially in the south of Germany. Article 106 of the Basic Law guarantees them certain revenues, although these revenues are generally thought to be insufficient to their functions.

The German city dweller in most *Lander* has the benefit of quarter-councils with powers and budgets resembling those of the French arrondisement councils, but with a somewhat more established position under *Lander* constitutions. In addition, the spreading popularity of traffic calming accords him some control of his immediate street environment not present in many other countries.

In Germany, small-scale government was restored as an act of policy by the occupying powers following World War II. They thus carried out for the occupied state a reform they failed to impose on their own institutions. Until the Nazi era, local government in Germany retained many of the characteristics of the medieval city-state, whose abolition came in Germany much later than in Britain and France. Postwar municipalities also gained unusual autonomy by reason of the fact that in the period from 1945 to 1949 they were the only popularly controlled level of government.

HISTORY OF THE GEMEINDE

The traditional unit of local government in Germany was the *Gemeinde*. Some 24,278 of these entities existed in 1968. While the importance of the gemeinde declined throughout the nineteenth century as the unification of Germany proceeded, many of the larger *Gemeinden* historically had been city-states, and the *Gemeinde* had an autonomy and constitutional position that municipalities had never been accorded in England or the United States. The dominant model was that of Baron Vom Stein's Prussian City Charter Law of 1808, which conceived of the city as an "autonomous corporation distinct from the state, the citizens of which were to take responsibility for administering themselves their own sphere of activities", Vom Stein's ideal being that

"Confidence ennobles man, continuous tutelage hampers his development, participation in public affairs brings with it a sense of political significance, and the greater this sense becomes, the greater also grow interest in the common good and the fascination of taking part in public activities, both of which elevate the nation's spirit."[1]

Under the Prussian Municipal Ordinance of 1808, citizens eligible to vote in local elections (male property owners over the age of 24, or about one sixth of the adult population) were liable for three years' service in the communal government, generally in connection with charities or poor relief, the punishment for refusal to accept office being loss of civic rights for three to six years and taxation on a higher scale. In 1831, the Prussian City Charter law was revised to substantially enhance state supervision, although cities were allowed to exempt themselves from it. Ensuing Prussian laws heavily weighted the municipal electorate toward property owners. In 1853, following the failure of the 1848 revolution, state supervision was enhanced. Nonetheless, down to World War I, German municipalities retained a substantial degree of self-government.

Article 127 of the Weimar Constitution guaranteed local governments the right to self-government "within the limits of the laws" but also provided for proportional representation on city councils. A high degree of state supervision prevailed, allowing displacement of mayors by state commissions. Under the Third Reich, city councils were reduced to advisory functions, and both mayors and councilors were appointed from above.

The Potsdam Agreement called for "decentralization of the political structure and the development of local responsibility . . . throughout Germany on democratic principles and in particular through elective councils." This contemplated restoration of the *Gemeinde* first, higher organs of government to be restored "as rapidly as may be justified by successful application of these principles in local self-government."[2] The result of this agreement was that there was a four-year period "between 1945 and 1949 when local governments were free of any state supervision [, which] strengthened dramatically the self-confidence of local officials . . . local self-government was to gain a place in German society which few other systems of local government could match."[3]

In the American and French zones, there was essentially a reversion to the pre-1933 system of local government. In the British zone, under the influence of Professor W. A. Robson, a system of local government that reduced the power of the burgermeister by placing administrative functions under a town clerk leading a nonpolitical civil service was put in place. This system survives in the important states of North Rhine-Westphalia and Lower Saxony. Police were also decentralized to the municipal level in the British zone, but control over them was returned to the land level after the end of the occupation.[4]

RECENT REFORMS

Of the 24,278 *Gemeinden* in 1968, 16,000 had less than 1,000 people, and only 1,200 had more than 5,000. The smaller municipalities delegated functions to neighboring municipalities or joint authorities, a practice viewed as having "undermined local self-government in the first instance and the principle of unity of administration in the second."[5] A consensus in favor of change arose, beginning at an annual meeting of German legal scholars in 1964. In general, it was felt that municipalities should not have less than 7,000 to 8,000 people (5,000 in Bavaria) and that in the case of larger municipalities, a two-tier system was in order, the object being to provide a basis for each municipality "again assum[ing] on its own as many tasks as possible."[6] In the final event, a number of *Lander* established federations of municipalities to create entities of the required size, the minimum size necessary for membership in such a federation ranging from 200 to 2,000. The result of the reforms between 1968 and 1978 was a reduction in the number of municipalities from 24,000 to 8,409, of which about 5,000 were federations of municipalities.

In the Social Democrat-controlled states, municipalities tended to be larger, and unitary municipalities prevailed. About 3,000 of the surviving entities had less than 1,000. In addition, districts (*Bezirke*) were to be formed in large cities and *Ortshaften* (villages) in the smaller unitary municipalities. The latter were to be coterminous with the newly annexed villages and were to have "elected councillors and a decentralized administrative apparatus--their power would be determined generally by the local general purpose government."[7]

The municipal laws of the important states of Bavaria, Hesse and North Rhine-Westphalia provide for the creation of submunicipal districts, as does that of Rheinland-Pfalz, and the independent cities of Berlin, Bremen, and Hamburg are respectively divided into 20, 14, and 7 subdistricts, each with its own council. Thus, the provisions of Section 82.3 of the laws of the State of Hessen provide for quarter-councils delineated by city bylaws following existing local communities, with elections at the same time as the city council, and further provides that:

[t]he quarter-council has to be heard as to all important matters concerning the quarter including the draft of the budget. It has the right to make proposals, and must comment in response to the City Council. The City Council may transfer rights of final decision

to quarter-councils if this does not endanger the unity of the municipality. The quarter-councils must get budgets adequate to their tasks.[8]

The size of the population served by quarter-councils varies greatly. There are eight quarter-councils in Frankfurt for a population of 680,000 and four in Konigstein for a population of 18,000. In Cologne, there are eight large districts (*Stadtteck*) with 10,000 to 150,000 persons each in which local administrative offices are organized, these boundaries also being used by the federal post office, taxing authorities, and state police; these, in turn, are divided into a total of 48 smaller districts (*Stadtbezerhe*), which are significant only for such purposes as the organization of carnival parades.[9] The size of municipalities in general is greatest in northern Germany, where Social Democratic governments had control, and smallest in Bavaria. In recent years, there has been a movement toward making the chairmanship of the council a popularly elected position in the northern states as well as in Bavaria and Wurtemberg, where this was the historic pattern.[10]

One consequence of the municipal reform is said to have been that "large city interests are now given more weight than the metropolitan periphery [in planning], an interesting contrast with the American scene."[11] In addition, municipalities were absolved from the requirement of advance clearance of their land use planning by District Councils; plans are now deemed automatically approved if not disapproved within three months. An additional result is said to be that "the citizen today is closer to a competent local bureaucracy in a position to make more important decisions."[12] On the other hand, the somewhat increased size of municipalities is said to have contributed to a greater politicization of elections in rural areas.

Unlike the municipalities, the *Bezirke* have no legal guarantee under Article 28 of the constitution of continued existence as institutions. Typically, they have been accorded "elected councils, some limited powers and in most cases a small administrative staff."[13] The irreducible powers of municipalities under Article 28 were affirmed in the 1983 *Rastede* decision of the Federal Administrative Court. In addition, an amendment to Article 106 of the Basic Law guaranteed certain revenues to the municipalities, including equalization payments.

The degree to which German government is decentralized, at least to the *Lander* level, is indicated by the statistics as to the number of employees at various levels of government. In 1980, there were 1.82 million employees of the *Lander*, 1.2 million in local government, and only 330,000 federal employees, in addition to 800,000 in the postal services and 340,000 in the railways. In addition, special-purpose authorities employed 40,000 persons; federal labor and social insurance offices, 134,000; and local social insurance offices, 92,000.[14]

STREET PEDESTRIANIZATION

Germany has been one of the leading countries in the organization of street pedestrianization schemes.[15] The German Federal Law of Urban Renewal of 1971 enhanced the role of both municipalities and their residents in urban renewal plans. Since then, traffic calming (known in Germany as *Verkehrsberuhigung*) and the creation of areas for joint use of traffic and pedestrians known as *Wohnberichten* have become major local questions in Germany. It has been noted that

[t]he difference between the European and North American attitudes can be linked to the fact that the urban tradition (appreciation and resultant use of urban amenities and institutions) has been and still continues to be much more deeply rooted in the European value system.[16]

Another writer has observed:

Open space is a scarce resource in a densely populated country like Germany. . . . As a result, traffic management, together with increased open space for play socialization and leisure, are seen as two essential components of the livability of existing neighborhoods. Traffic plans are developed for entire residential precincts to eliminate through traffic and to reduce driving speeds. The means used to implement these plans include erecting traffic barriers at intersections, cul-de-sacs or one-way streets, and slowing traffic by building humps or bumps, elevating intersections, or narrowing traffic lanes.[17]

The same writer lists a number of studies of the effects of the German *Wohberichten*, which were modelled on Dutch areas known as *Woonerven*.[18] The German developments began on a large scale in North Rhine-Westphalia in 1976. It was found that the new zones produced a 20% decline in accidents and a 50% decline in severe accidents. "By the end of the 1980's skepticism of the traditional traffic engineers about traffic calming has still not completely disappeared and many would like not to apply it, but there is tremendous pressure by the population to apply traffic calming."[19]

Germany remains a country in which, despite the density of the population, 29% of the land area is forests and 55% is farmland. The heavy use of special assessments also may operate to discourage sprawl development. "When [a] public investment is constructed, the affected landowners must contribute part of the cost, according to formulas based on the increase in the value of their land."[20]

The Dutch schemes "invited the residents who were living in those streets which were to be redesigned to participate and express their own ideas . . . an integration into one road surface [of sidewalk and road areas] was to be provided giving the visual impression of a residential yard."[21] By 1980, four years after the authorization of *Woonerven* in Holland, 260 of 800 local authorities had adopted them. The Dutch scheme allowed neighborhoods to petition for *Woonerfs* by a 60% vote at a meeting attended by a majority of neighborhood citizens, so long as nondivertible traffic is not affected and adequate parking is provided. The traffic rules applicable in *Woonerfs* are the following:

Pedestrians may use the full width of the road within an area defined as a woonerf; playing on the roadway is also permitted. Drivers within a woonerf may not drive faster than [9 to 12 mph]. They must make allowance for the possible presence of pedestrians, children at play, unmarked objects. . . . [T]raffic approaching from the right at whatever speed always has priority. Drivers may not impede pedestrians. Pedestrians may not unreasonably hinder the progress of drivers.[22]

"This practice is characterized by decentralized decision-making with a freedom from central government controls and flexible incremental implementation involving genuine public participation."[23]

REPLATTING OF BLOCKS

By reason of the traditional lack of both primogeniture and freedom of testation in German law, and consequent fragmentation of properties, German law has traditionally made liberal provision for the replatting and reorganization of lots. With respect to agricultural lands, a federal law, the Flurbereinigungsgesetz, contains provisions on amicable arrangements for the reparceling of agricultural areas by agreement to ensure better use of labor and machinery, and the antecedent state laws date to at least 1895.[24] With respect to urban areas, a considerable degree of neighborhood planning was achieved through the practice of municipal land banking, including "the provision of leasehold land for nonprofit housing . . . regulating not only the supply of land but also the extent and form in which it might be developed."[25] Thus, by 1900, the City of Berlin owned 34.8% of the land within its boundaries, and by 1906, 50% of the land in Frankfurt and 77.7% of that in Freiburg was municipally owned.

In 1905, an English commentator described the provisions of the Saxon Building Law, Section 54 of which provided:

For the purpose of obtaining convenient sites for buildings, a repartition of the area can be made, even against the will of the owners, by an alteration of the boundaries of the plots, or by redistribution in case the new arrangement is in the public interest and a request to that effect is made to the Building-police authority either a) by the Town

Council or b) by more than half of the interested owners of land who together own more than half the land in question.[26]

Under the scheme, plots that were unimproved but used in an unusual way, such as gardens and nurseries, might be excluded but might also be subjected to boundary rectifications. Upon institution of the scheme, a two-year moratorium against erection of new buildings rendering redistribution more difficult, applied. Upon redistribution, the prior owners received shares in the newly plotted land proportionate to their shares in the land as previously plotted. Lots with buildings were restored to the owners with appropriate boundary rectifications. Unavoidable differences in value might be settled in money, and lots of unbuildable size were subject to compulsory sale, the funds for compensation being recovered from the remaining owners.

This scheme was popularly known as the Lex Adickes after its principal sponsor, the burgermeister of Frankfurt, who agitated for it for nearly a decade until its adoption in that city in 1902. It was generalized to Prussia after World War I and was adopted in Baden and Saxony well before it and schemes like it are said to have been successfully applied in connection with the postwar reconstruction of both Kiel and Rotterdam.[27] As to Frankfurt:

[i]t is significant that the mere possession of the power to compel unwilling owners to come into the pool made its application unnecessary. During the first ten years 14 areas with a total extent of 375 acres were pooled and redistributed, with the assent of the owners. Originally consisting of 643 lots belonging to 149 different owners, the land was reparcelled into 198 after a deduction ranging from 25 to 40 per cent for street purposes and the greater part of the land is now built upon.[28]

The British *Uthwatt Report on Compensation and Betterment* (Cmd. 6386, 1942) rejected the Adickes plan on the basis that:

[t]he responsible authority would need to take over and demolish the property in the area, presumably paying compensation for the buildings, and then hand back the bare sites to a large number of separate owners, some of whom might have neither the desire nor the capital to rebuild. The division into the fixed number of sites might be prejudicial to proper replanning, and in any event it would not provide a permanent solution to the problem which large-scale ownership creates. (Par. 143)

Rejoining, a defender of the plan observed:

If an obsolescence tax operated, those who had "neither the desire nor the capital" would already have sold out to someone who had. There would be no need for a division into a fixed number of sites; former owners would get shares according to an Inland Revenue valuation of the site alone, of value say 50 [pounds] each, with which they would have first preference to buy a number of new sites (with appropriate planning permission) or developed buildings. If they wanted neither, they could sell the shares for money.[29]

In place of this system, the characteristic American method of land assembly has involved condemnation of the entire area, including the viable buildings, an approach held permissible by the Supreme Court in *Berman v. Parker* but leading to great expense and delay and the frequent blighting of neighborhoods while improvements proceed.[30]

Two other devices for neighborhood construction were introduced in early German practice. The first was a scheme embodied in Section 40 of the Saxon Building Law similar to American requirements of open space dedication in suburban developments, pursuant to which an urban developer

must sell to [the] town any land . . . which forms part of the inner portion of the square. For the rest, the community has to obtain and put in order the center of the square. The square must be put in order, at the latest, when the streets surrounding it are completed, all the area of the square is obtained, and at least a third the circumference of the square has been built upon.[31]

Section 90 of the Saxon Building Law also constituted an early example of historical preservation: "Buildings which form a public disfigurement may be prohibited . . . [H]igher architectural demands can be made for certain streets or parts of streets in respect of the buildings to be erected there."[32]

HOUSING PROJECTS

Early German social housing, to a greater degree than its counterparts in other countries, provided for a tenant role in management. Much housing was built under an 1889 Prussian law granting concessions to cooperative housing societies. The pre-1910 schemes of the Berlin Building and Savings Society provided for choice by the tenants of "a housemaster who collects the rents, watches the premises, and represents the tenants before the Board of Directors."[33] Similarly, the Joint Stock Company for Small Dwellings in Frankfurt provided that:

[t]he tenants of each of the larger houses choose a representative and the representatives take part with the managers in settling disputes among the tenants. Coals and potatoes are bought at wholesale prices for the tenants. The services of housekeepers can be obtained. . . . For some of the youngest children there is a creche.[34]

With respect to the poorest housing, a variant of the late nineteenth-century English and American practice of "friendly visiting" was in effect before the First World War, known as the Elberfeld system,[35] pursuant to which five or ten families were placed under the care of a member of the well-to-do class for a period of three years. Approximately one fifth of 1% of the population is said to have rendered service in this fashion, the service being theoretically compulsory for at least some of the upper classes voting in the three-class system based on property then used in German municipal elections. This conception of the duties of citizenship survives in provisions in Berlin, Hamburg, Bremen, and Hesse, which confide certain functions of municipal government to *Deputationen* made up partly of elected councilors and partly of co-opted citizens to supervise schools and other community institutions.

These elaborate schemes, which affected only a small portion of the housing stock, are reflected in more recent creation of neighborhood development foundations in the state of Hesse, which accord residents of social housing the right to select new tenants from lists of three proposed tenants put forth by the Housing Authority.[36]

The reconstruction of high-rise flats has likewise been of interest in Germany. While a study showed no direct correlation between architectural design and crime rate, this may have been a function of the low general crime rate:

"[A]lmost no crimes were committed in semi-private building areas such as halls and stairwells: a welcome finding which contrasts with the situation in the U.S.A. [However,] the interaction among residents was far more intense in multiple dwellings than in high-rises; interaction was greater in buildings with defensible space than in those without . . . the residents of high-rises were more afraid of being victimized than those in multiple dwellings.[37]

In Hamburg, a program to upgrade a district includes:

1. Improving recreational activities for children and young people by setting up playgrounds, club houses, athletic grounds, and workshops.

2. Creating places for people to get together (cafes, women's centers, party centers).

3. Providing various advisory services for the residents of large developments such as schools for parents, advice on further education, contacts for families of other nationalities, and financial advice from consumer associations.

4. [A]bolishing the income limit stipulated in the Housing Allocation Act for new tenants.

5. Improving the standard of target hardening.[38]

NEIGHBORHOOD RENEWAL

Under a 1982 act of the Berlin Parliament, homeowners organizing self-help projects and contributing 15% of the costs may receive construction assistance of DM800 per square meter. Approximately DM26 million was distributed to 40 groups under this program in 1984. A second program pays approximately 70% of material costs in connection with small self-help projects, approximately DM5 million being made available for 1,000 such projects in 1984.[39]

NOTES

1. See A. Gunlicks, *Local Government in the German Federal System* (1986), at 9. The second quotation is from a memorandum written for Vom Stein by the Konigsburg police director, J. G. Frey. See R. Hiscocks, *Democracy in Western Germany* (1957), at 172. For an appreciation of Vom Stein's municipal reforms, see F. Meinecke, *The Age of German Liberation, 1795-1815* (1977), at 74-79. For excerpts from the ordinance, see J. Seeley, 2 *Life and Times of Stein* (1878), at 238-43. See generally M. Walker, *German Home Towns* (1971).

2. Potsdam Agreement, sec. 2, par. 9.

3. Gunlicks, *supra* note 1, at 30.

4. *Id.* at 28. See W. Robson, *Local Government in Occupied Germany*, 16 Political Quarterly (1945), at 277-87.

5. Gunlicks, *supra* note 1 at 28.

6. *Id.* at 52.

7. *Id.*

8. Fuhr and Pfeil, Laws of Hessen, section 823. Informal verbal translation by Prof. Eckard Rehbinder. See generally R. Hiscocks, *supra* note 1; R. Chaput de Saintonge, *Public Administration in Germany* (1961), at 143-44. In his City Planning report to General Clay, Walter Gropius, the emigre architect, recommended breaking up cities into

"small neighborhood units, in which the essential importance of the individual can be realized, his needs met and his voice heard." The influence of this report is unclear. See J. Diefendorf, *The Rebuilding of Urban Germany*, in *American Policy and the Reconstruction of West Germany 1945-55* (H. Lehmann ed. 1993), at 331, 335 n.10, and works there cited.

9. L. Fischer, *Cologne*, in *Great Cities of the World* (2d ed. W. Robson ed. 1957). On similar councils in Rotterdam, see R. Morlan, *Sub-Municipal Government in Practice: The Rotterdam Experience*, 35 Western Political Quarterly 425 (1982); in Bologna, see F. Bandarsin, *The Bologna Experience*, in *The Conservation of European Cities* (D. Appleyard ed. 1979), at 178, 191. In Bologna, the councils administer elementary schools, child care centers, and branch libraries under central supervision. See also R. Nanetti, *From the Top Down: Government-Promoted Citizen Participation*, 9 Journal of Volunteer Action Research 149 (1980).

10. Gunlicks, *supra* note 7.

11. A. Hooper, *Development Control in the Federal Republic of Germany*, 59 Town Planning Review 198 (1988).

12. Gunlicks, *supra* note 7, at 63.

13. *Id.* at 31. On irreducible municipal powers, see H. Uppendahl, *Intergovernmental Relations in the Federal Republic of Germany*, in *The Present and Future Role of Local Government in Great Britain and the Federal Republic of Germany* (1985), at 35-48. On revenue sharing, see the quotations from the Basic Law in C. Schweitzer, *Politics and Government in the Federal Republic of Germany: Basic Documents* (1984), at 173-75; B. Weinberger, *Local Government Taxes in Germany and Their Future*, 3 Studies in Comparative Local Government, no. 2 (1969), at 25-28.

14. Gunlicks, *supra* note 1, at 144.

15. C. Hass-Klau, *The Pedestrian and City Traffic* (1990).

16. N. Pressman, *The European Experience*, in *Public Streets for Public Use* (A. Moudon ed. 1987), at 40, 43. See G. Wynne, *Learning from Abroad, Traffic Restraints in Residential Neighborhoods* (1980).

17. B. Eubank-Ahrens, *A Closer Look at the Users of Woonerven*, in *Public Streets for Public Use* (A. Moudon ed. 1987), at 63. See also J. Kray, *Woonerven and Other Experiments in the Netherlands*, 12 Built Environment 20 (1986).

18. Eubank-Ahrens, *supra* note 17, at 79.

19. C. Hass-Klau, *supra* note 15, at 223. See P. Barnes, *Environmental Traffic Restraint: German Approaches to Traffic Management by Design*, 12 Built Environment 60 (1986).

20. T. Schoenbrun, *Planning and Land Development Law in the Federal Republic of Germany*, 54 Tulane Law Review 624 (1980).

21. Hass-Klau, *supra* note 15, at 212.

22. D. Appleyard, *Liveable Streets* (1981), at 249-51. See T. Pharaoh and J. Russell, *Traffic Calming Policy and Performance: The Netherlands, Denmark, and Germany*, 62 Town Planning Review 79 (1991), Organization for Economic Cooperation and Development, *Traffic Safety in Residential Areas* (1979).

23. J. Russell, *Viewpoint: Traffic Calming and Town Planning*, 61 Town Planning Review iii (1990).

24. O. Kimminich, *Public Participation in the Federal Republic of Germany*, 53 Town Planning Review 274, 278 (1982). See T. Horsfall, *The Improvement of the Dwelling and Surroundings of the People: The Example of Germany* (1905), at 60.

25. N. Bullock and J. Read, *The Movement for Housing Reform in Germany and France 1840-1914* (1985) at 7.

26. Horsfall, supra note 24, at 41. For another description, see *Royal Commission on the Distribution of Industrial Population* (Cmd. 6153) (1940), par. 257-61. See also H. Lunn, *Municipal Lessons from Southern Germany* (1908), at ch. 4; J. Rollins, *Liberals, Socialists and City Government in Imperial Germany* (1979).

27. As to Rotterdam, see L. Mumford, *The City in History* (1961), at 424; as to Kiel, see P. Hall, *London 2000* (1963), at 233; E. Greene, *West German City Reconstruction: Two Case Studies*, 7 Social Review (N.S.) 231 (1959).

28. W. Dawson, *Municipal Life and Government in Germany* (1916).

29. P. Hall, *supra note 27*, at 233. On participation of landowners and occupants in the decision and execution of contemporary urban renewal schemes, see Kimminich, *supra* note 24, at 277.

30. See M. Anderson, *The Federal Bulldozer* (1967).

31. Horsfall, *supra* note 24, at 68.

32. *Id.*

33. F. Howe, *European Cities at Work* (1913), at 167.

34. Horsfall, *supra* note 24, at 161.

35. See *id.* at 173; J. Sutter, *Britain's Next Campaign* (1903). On *Deputationen*, see Meinecke, *supra* note 1, at 78; Hiscocks, *supra* note 1, at 178; W.Dawson, *Municipal Life and Government in Germany* (2d ed. 1916), at 97-99.

36. M. Harloe, *New Ideas for Housing: The Experience of Three Countries* (1990), at 30.

37. E. Kube, *Architecture and Crime Prevention*, in *Police Research in the Federal Republic of Germany* (E. Kube ed. 1991), ch. 9.

38. *Id.*

39. C. Hass-Klau, *Soft Urban Renewal in Krenzburg*, 12 Built Environment 165, 172 (1986).

4

The United States—Free Market Governments

The American town dweller exerts limited political control over his municipal government. In most parts of the country, the growth in population since town boundaries were determined or the use of county government ensures that the typical resident is submerged in a large political entity. Even school districts, once quite small, have been consolidated into large units, and their powers and finances are so circumscribed by state law that local control is limited. It is only where new developments have been created, employing private residential community associations, that neighborhood government can be said to be a reality.

In American cities, no entity similar to the residential community association has appeared, and general-purpose submunicipal governments do not exist. The creation of new special districts within existing municipal boundaries is precluded by statute, and new development of any kind is legally difficult. Cities have thus deteriorated in their social and civic vitality.

For James Bryce,[1] the degraded state of municipal and local government was the gravest failure of the American polity. It is striking, and perhaps appropriate, that the revival of civic institutions has not come about by reason of any discussion among the opportunistic and centralizing political class, but rather as a result of private market arrangements designed to maximize the value and security of land.

TOWNS IN AMERICA

Although the 13 original American colonies were founded pursuant to various forms of royal grant and charter, their internal organization rapidly assumed two distinctive forms. In the North, settlers organized townships, frequently in areas six miles square. A great many early townships were religious communities, founded by express covenants, such as that described by Governor John Winthrop of the Plymouth Colony in his Model of Christian Charity to make others' conditions our own, rejoice together, always having before our eyes our commission and community in the work, our community as members of the same bond. These communities in New England have been described as "the most intense community experience of modern times." . . . . [I]n the absence of true communities we would have witnessed the re-creation of European peasants and landlords.[2]

In the plantation states of the South where slaveholding was common, counties of varying size were erected; in many states, the present alignment of counties was substantially in place by the end of the seventeenth century. The virtues of the township as being an entity of sufficient size to allow landowners to possess both village houses and fields have been expanded upon by many commentators, particularly those associated with the "garden city" movement,[3] the analogy being drawn to the ideal of Plato's Laws, in which each citizen owned two lots, one at the center and one at the periphery of the city.[4]

Around the common, from the very outset, the public buildings were erected: the meeting house, the town hall, and later the school. . . . . [t]he common did duty as drill ground for the local militia, another medieval institution. The political importance of this new form must not be underrated, though the failure to grasp it and to continue it--indeed to incorporate it in both the Federal and State Constitution--was one of the tragic oversights of post revolutionary political development.[5]

The town system, and particularly the direct democracy of early meetings, was celebrated by de Tocqueville and by Emerson. The latter, referring to the voluntary association characteristic of the settlement of the American West, observed "they are all skillful in California, or on Robinson Crusoe's Island, instantly to erect a working government, as the French and Germans are not [elsewhere] the town system is not the base, and therefore the expenditure of the legislature is not economic but prodigal."[6] As late as 1982, the minimum number of persons necessary to establish a new municipal corporation was "75 in Alabama, 100 in Nebraska, New Mexico, Oregon and Wisconsin, 200 in Tennessee and 250 in Nevada."[7]

Today town government involving direct democracy survives only in northern New England. The populations of the originally established townships now frequently number in the tens or hundreds of thousands, and their borders, generally laid out in straight lines in both New England and the Midwest, are as arbitrary under modern conditions as the more undulating boundaries of British towns referred to by H. G. Wells as "a boundary line determined by mapping out the wanderings of an intoxicated excursionist."[8] Much has been made in recent years of the fact that cities and towns are deemed creatures of the state, lacking even the limited protection under the Constitution accorded private corporations,[9] although the diminution of constitutional immunity has been accompanied in most states by the grant to municipalities of "home rule" powers sung well beyond their original charters, nullifying the alleged malign effects of Dillon's Rule that "any fair reasonable doubt concerning the existence of power is resolved by the courts against the municipal corporation, and the power is denied."[10]

Thus, because of the great size of many townships and municipalities, their nonexistence in many parts of the country, and the dysfunctional limits on their jurisdiction, imposed by restrictive annexation laws, as well as their lack of social or economic homogeneity, the typical American town does not meet the conditions for direct democracy recognized by Rousseau.[11] He observed:

[i]n the first place the State must be sufficiently small to make it possible to call the whole people together without difficulty and each citizen must be in a position to know all his neighbors. In the second place, manners must be so simple that business will be kept to a minimum and thorny questions avoided. There should be, too, considerable equality in fortune and rank, for otherwise there will not long be equality in rights and authority. Finally, there must be little or no luxury, because . . . it corrupts both the rich and the poor, the rich through their possessions, the poor through their lust to possess.[12]

American towns are thus not British parish councils or French communes. For practical purposes, they are irrelevant to our inquiry.

"NEIGHBORHOOD" IN THE 1960s

Similarly irrelevant, as akin to utopian communities, are the surviving "neighborhood" groups organized under the auspices of the War on Poverty of the late 1960s. The neighborhoods concerned were typically neighborhoods of 50,000 to 100,000 and were designed not to provide grass-roots participation (notwithstanding contrary pretense) but to co-opt or create a political class and provide "inter unit competition in the quality of services, which is lacking in large cities."[13]

"The people had to 'participate' in their democracy in a very special way, i.e. through 'social conflict'. What these social critics had in mind was no reconstituted New England town meeting of any kind: *that* was a vehicle for consensus." " . . . the institutions used to facilitate community participation were not the actual institutions of the community but were created by those in charge of the program."[14] When the fruits of this experiment were examined, it was found that "only in block associations, with a 'community' size of several hundred--did widespread citizen participation occur--decentralization will not advance the town meeting ideal of participatory democracy unless the community involved is extremely small."[15]

Even these relatively few block experiments were suspect--given the confessed paternalism of the entire project: "[t]he community organization movement has transferred the principal burdens of leadership into the hands of professionals. This . . . is an extraordinary development especially in a society that has so thoroughly identified leadership in public affairs with the amateur or elected official."[16]

We thus must direct our attention to other less fashionable and less recognized manifestations of small community organization in American law. Preeminent among these are the residential community associations and condominium associations created in large numbers in the last several decades. Before discussing these, however, some less conspicuous legal manifestations of small community organization deserve to be considered.

STREET CLOSING REGIMES

Among these are the traditional American regime relating to the improvement and closing of streets, a subject lent great importance by the fact that most American cities were laid out, to their probable detriment, on the open grid pattern. "By usually failing to discriminate sufficiently in the first instance between main traffic arteries and residential streets, the first were not made wide enough while the second were usually too wide for purely neighborhood functions."[17] This excess "threw the costs of extra paving and over-lengthy utilities lines and mains upon residential streets that could ill afford them."[18] "The undifferentiated rectangular plan of Manhattan, a plan contrived as if for the purpose of keeping neighborhoods from coming into existence, . . . without pubs or plazas lacked a center, provided no fixed boundaries for neighborhoods."[19]

Traditionally, "compensation for the land taken for streets was to be raised as an assessment on the surrounding property benefited by the laying out of streets."[20] The usefulness of the special assessment procedure was significantly impaired in 1907 by a Supreme Court decision holding that assessments could not be proportioned to damages caused by the property owner remedied by the public project but only to benefits conferred by it.[21] This early decision, reinforced by the recent Supreme Court decisions in the *Loretto* and *Nollan* cases renewing the principle, limits the power of the state to replat and reallocate lots and close streets without substantial expense.

A survey of American law reveals early forms of street government by neighboring owners such as an early District of Columbia statute[22] allowing alleys to be closed "upon petition of the owners of more than one-half the real estate in the square." It was suggested as early as 1907 that:

[I]t would cost very little for the city to purchase some of the large alleys outright and convert them into places of resort or amusement. It would also be profitable for private property owners to treat an entire square as a unit by developing, in its center, grass plots, flowers, shade trees, benches, walks, places for drying clothes, facilities for children's play and a bandstand for local concerts, all to be used and paid for in increased rentals, by the residents of dwelling houses and apartment buildings around the square.[23]

This suggestion for the replatting of urban blocks in a fashion reminiscent of the Lex Adickes in early twentieth-century Frankfurt did not find general acceptance, though it was echoed 80 years later in Dolores Hayden's proposals for the similar replatting for community use of the interior of suburban blocks.[24] These suggestions were resisted when originally made on the basis of police fears of "little fenced off communities where the moral order of the outside streets could not be well enforced," the self-policing nature of such communities being ignored.[25]

Similar suggestions have been made by others. Thus, the closing and replatting of streets as well as interior blocks has been urged on the basis that "streets are 'the great urban outdoors,' the publicly controlled land bank that American cities have always lacked."[26] The general rule in the United States is that "in cases of multiple abutting owners local statutes usually require the approval of at least a majority of the owners to vacate the street."[27] The benefits seen as flowing from the privatization of streets are

[i]ncome from the sale; return of the property to the tax rolls; employment generated both by construction and by the occupants; elimination of the municipality's liability and reduction of public maintenance responsibilities.[28]

It has been suggested that as long as an easement is left for emergency vehicle access and for utilities that the municipal costs involved in closings are minimal, and the benefits to neighboring landowners can be recovered either through square-foot benefit assessments or from a general reassessment of the values of neighboring properties. The only detriment is found in the fact that "discontinuities in grid layout tend to isolate communities by impeding local access."[29] That this may not in fact be a detriment is suggested by recent developments in Chicago and other cities in which barriers and cul-de-sacs have been created at the request of street residents to increase community control over crime.

STREET PRIVATIZATION

In at least two American cities, there has been substantial privatization of streets. Early developments of this type took place in St. Louis County, through the use of indentures by which title to the bed of a street is deeded to the residents adjacent to it, subject to assessments enforceable by lien.[30] The affairs of the associations are governed by trustees elected at an annual meeting. As of 1986, there were no less than 427 street-providing subdivisions in St. Louis County, the typical subdivision having between 21 and 102 homes. Ninety percent of the street associations provided street repair and sewer removal; more than 30% assume responsibility for sweeping, mowing, tree trimming, or street lighting; and more than a third obstruct access to one end of a street. "Barriers are agreed upon by neighborhood associations on both sides of the barrier."[31] Fifteen percent provide nonstreet services such as a security patrol. The mean annual assessment was $103 in 1986.[32] Residents of the area received a small tax abatement for maintaining the right of way.

While the St. Louis County streets are in long-established and prosperous suburban districts, more recent developments in more modest neighborhoods have taken place in the city of St. Louis with considerable success[33] and legislation has permitted privatization on less-than-unanimous consent, on petition of 95% of residents.[34] A more modest effort in St. Louis permits street closing on local petition without privatization of street beds. Where streets are privatized, they cannot be reopened by a municipality without recourse to eminent domain or the grant of an easement.

A second illustration of street privatization is supplied by recent developments in Laredo, Texas, where sale of streets may be initiated either by the city or adjacent landowners, who are given a right of veto and a right of first refusal to acquire the adjacent street bed. Existing streets are replatted to ensure that each property has street access. This has led observers to suggest that cities

beg[i]n to seek actively to tighten the entire network of streets they own with the objective not only of saving money in upkeep, but of providing opportunities for additional parking, open space and so forth. . . . [T]he advantages for the communities buying the lots would be control of a large portion of the right of way including parking [and] planting. . . . [P]rivate citizens are represented on "parks boards" yet few communities have advisory citizen "street boards."[35]

It may be recalled that Los Angeles was once characterized as "the city of vacant lots: areas subdivided fifty years ago still stand idle, yet require expensive municipal services."[36] Even more broadly, it has been suggested:

The concept of the amenity cooperative could be applied to the urban street at two scales. The most obvious is the sale of a particular street, or segment of a street. Property-owners, if convinced that a particular amenity is desirable, could cooperatively develop such an amenity, own it, and maintain it. Examples such as shopping arcades, shuttle bus services, and even landscape planning and good lighting come to mind. . . . [B]enefit assessment is an existing and working example of such a procedure. A mechanism of real estate tax abatements on improvements and value added by the amenity, as well as special depreciation write-off schedules, might be combined as a public subsidy to such voluntary cooperatives.

At the wider scale, all property owners along streets would be considered required members of amenity cooperatives. . . . To a greater or lesser degree, public subsidy could be granted depending on detailed correlation and determination of public interest improvements provided by and perhaps required of the amenity cooperative. Preferential treatment to capital expenditures for approved street development, if properly rewarded, could lead to far-flung private programs to improve street quality according to revised concepts.[37]

The paradox is that a form of privatization is needed in order for city streets, at least, to fulfil the function of public property identified by Carol Rose:

In the absence of the socializing activities that take place on "inherently public property," the public is a shapeless mob, whose members neither trade nor converse nor play, but only fight, in a setting where life is, in Hobbes' all too famous phrase, solitary, poor, nasty, brutish and short.[38]

AMENITY COOPERATIVES

American experience provides a number of illustrations of the creation of amenity cooperatives for the creation and maintenance of park lands. The earliest of these were the associations established by deed covenants in 1831 to maintain Gramercy Park in New York and in 1844 to maintain Louisburg Square in Boston. More recent examples include a Minneapolis procedure allowing 51% of neighboring property owners to seek creation of a new park. When the petition is allowed, the park is created and the neighbors are constituted an assessment district for its maintenance.[39] Various state laws allow grant of land for gardens to "incorporated or unincorporated associations, including neighborhood or block associations," as in New York;[40] permit grants to community associations for historic presentation or community forestry as in Indiana,[41] or permit associations created by deed covenants the power to expand beyond the original common areas by acquiring park land, as in Florida.[42] A "neighborhood park" movement has generated a considerable literature.[43]

The creation of amenity cooperatives for the maintenance of day care centers was suggested by the Advisory Commission on Intergovernmental Relations as early as 1967, when it was suggested that neighborhood units of government be allowed to impose fractional millage on local property taxes, or a per capita tax, for, among other purposes, "after school programs for neighborhood children."[44] This approach has found limited favor by reason of the heavy interest of existing education and welfare bureaucracies in gaining control of day care centers.[45] The provision of tax credits to parents in the compromise federal legislation enacted in 1990[46] gave new impetus to efforts to organize neighborhood day care. As of 1991, the states of California, Connecticut, Florida, Massachusetts, Michigan, Minnesota, Montana, New Jersey, New York, Ohio, Oregon, Vermont, and Wisconsin had expressly preempted zoning restrictions against day care centers, and the states of California, Indiana, North Carolina, and Wisconsin had endeavored to invalidate private restrictions[47] against day care centers imposed by deed covenants. The most recent draft of the American Law Institute's Restatement of Servitudes[48] urges that covenants be construed to render day care a permitted residential use. Direct neighborhood control over this issue is provided in Maryland by a statute stating that covenants prohibiting business activity are not to be construed as prohibiting family day care centers unless a majority of all eligible association or condominium voters so declares. The association voters may limit the number of such facilities, but not to a number less than 7.5% of all units, and may impose a charge up to $50 for the use of common areas.[49]

THE "SOCIAL UNIT" EXPERIMENT

The most ambitious effort at neighborhood organization of a community social service was undertaken in Cincinnati in 1915 by a National Social Unit Organization presided over by Gifford Pinchot that attempted to organize communities at the block level for the purpose of delivering infant welfare services, prenatal services to mothers, and eventually preventative medical examination of adults with the aid of stipended block workers. Public meetings were held in each block in a section of Cincinnati for the purpose of electing block councils, which in turn elected a stipended block worker. The system foundered at the end of the war by reason of general public fear of socialism.[50] Less formal efforts to organize maternity health care at the neighborhood level took place under the Sheppard-Towner Maternity Care Act, the first American experiment in socialized medicine, from its enactment in the early 1920s to its repeal during the Hoover administration.[51]

SCHOOLS AND NEIGHBORHOODS

Although the original inspiration for public education in America was Jefferson's design for ward government, its development was heavily dependent on direction from the state level, beginning with the law in Massachusetts secured by Horace Mann. State law has exercised a compelling, and frequently malign, influence over such matters as the consolidation of small school districts, the certification of teachers, and collective bargaining and the resulting deprofessionalization of the teaching force. Recently, dissatisfaction with the size of schools and systems, with their excessive use for purposes of social integration, and with the quality of teaching, has led to a variety of schemes for enhanced community control as well as for more drastic forms of market-based decentralization such as voucher systems.

Jefferson's design for ward government contemplated three years of free education in primary schools of 40 students, each erected by taxation or compelled labor by a ward of five or six square miles with a population of about 500.

At every of those schools shall be taught reading, writing and common arithmetic and the books which shall be used therein for teaching children to read shall be such as will at the same time make them acquainted with Grecian, Roman, English and American history. History . . . will enable them to know ambition under whatever guise it may assume, and, knowing it, to defeat its views.[52]

Although the higher reaches of Jefferson's system, with its keystone the University of Virginia, contemplated a great measure of state involvement, the system of early education that developed bears little resemblance to that of his design. Some interest in the fuller integration of school and community arose in the 1920s with proposals for community centers in school buildings.[53] These left an impact on architecture if not on educational practice: "[t]he minimum requirements for a community center have now become a standard part of school design in almost every part of the United States."[54]

With the "school busing" controversies of the 1960s and 1970s, renewed attention was paid to the neighborhood basis of education. The busing experiment was described by sociologists of unquestioned disinterestedness as "profound sociological folly"[55] and as "destroying public responsibility and activity in a realm [schooling] that is traditionally associated with vigorous neighborhood civic activity."[56] The Congress "declare[d] it to be the policy of the United States that . . . the neighborhood is the appropriate basis for determining public school assignments."[57] The fruits of this interest are thus far limited. Congress has enacted a statute recognizing the role of secondary schools as community fora.[58] There have been provisions for school-based management in Hawaii; for neighborhood advisory councils in California; Florida, and South Carolina; and for governance of at least one Kentucky school in each school district by a council consisting of three teachers, two parents, and the principal.[59]

SPECIAL DISTRICTS

Another form of submunicipal government finding increasing use is the special zoning district with its own enforcement commission. Although special districts of various kinds have long been freely created in most states, in some, upon petition of landowners,[60] the new zoning districts are generally the product of legislative action. "The spreading use of historic districts also often involves a subterfuge of historic significance. The real purpose is to obtain a new regulatory mechanism for the neighborhood, similar to private mechanisms that can be exercised by neighborhood residents with much greater discretion than traditional zoning allows."[61]

Although the use of such districts has been criticized, on the basis that their prevention of dilapidation and mandated improvement of properties drives low-income groups out of neighborhoods as rents and tax assessments rise,[62] a similar complaint could be directed against any scheme for neighborhood improvements. In fact, it is open to almost any neighborhood to seek special zoning treatment, as the experience of many far-from-wealthy New York City neighborhoods attests.[63]

The typical historic district, to be sure, is not of street or block size, though in some instances its population is limited to several thousand, and the popularity of the device, which allows supervision of maintenance and aesthetic controls going beyond those of conventional zoning, is in no small measure due to the fact that the commission administering the restrictions has a neighborhood base.

A commercial analogue of the historic district is the business improvement district (BID) by which city councils in some large American cities, including Philadelphia and Baltimore, have designated improvement districts in downtown areas governed by boards selected by property owners with authority to impose a small (5 to 10%) surcharge on property taxes to be used to supplement the municipality's street cleaning, decorating, and policing efforts in downtown business districts.

RESIDENTIAL COMMUNITY ASSOCIATIONS

This discursive discussion of public sector developments leads to consideration of the most truly significant development in American local government: the rise of the residential community association. While in Britain, "the problems surrounding the enforcement of positive covenants have severely restricted freehold flat [and similar] development,"[64] and while in France these forms of development are said to be concentrated in resort areas,[65] American case law has vitiated this problem.[66]

The residential community association is a recent development. While the use of servitudes to organize community associates has been possible since the landmark case of *Tulk v. Moxhay*, 41 Eng. Rep. 1143 (Ch. 1848), and some associations, including those for Louisburg Square and Gramercy Park, antedate that decision,[67] their widespread use is a recent phenomenon. Some Frederick Olmstead-inspired developments, such as Roland Park in Baltimore, made use of servitudes to fund alley repairs early in this century, and the National Association of Real Estate Boards promoted their use, together with restrictive racial covenants until these were declared unconstitutional in 1948.[68] The number of associations in existence in 1960-62 was variously estimated at between 500 and 800. Private organizations, such as the National Association of Home Builders and the Urban Land Institute as well as some academics, published manuals recommending community association development in 1950,[69] but the real impetus for creation of associations began with enactment of Section 234 of the Housing Act of 1961 authorizing Federal Housing Administration (FHA) insurance of condominium mortgages and publication of a handbook by the principal federal mortgage lending agency, the FHA, in 1963.[70]

By 1988, it was estimated that there were as many as 130,000 residential community associations in the United States covering some 29 million people, approximately 12% of the nation's population.[71] It has been estimated that 70% of all new housing built in San Diego and Los Angeles Counties was part of a community association.[72] While 55% of the associations take the condominium form, the types of building involved are diverse: 15%, detached housing; 39%, townhouse; 16%, midrise; 99%, highrise; and 20%, mixed. The average size of associations has been variously described as 537 or 543 units--the median, a more modest 153. The average association fee was $867; the median fee was $336.

While Robert Wood wrote derisively in 1958 of "observers [who] seem to cherish the hope that in the suburbs we can recreate the small communities we have lost in our industrial sprawl since the Civil War,"[73] the new communities typically have assumed significant functions:

[t]heir natural history was to organize initially to deal with common problems the homeowners had with the developers; next to take on the township, the county, or whoever was supposed to provide local government services; then to sponsor recreation activities for children; and otherwise to become mostly dormant until some threat to tranquillity arose.[74]

A survey of member associations conducted by the Community Associations Institute revealed that 94% of the associations rendered outdoor maintenance services, 72% were responsible for trash collection, between 48% and 77% repaired streets and removed snow in addition to traffic-related functions, 31% maintained security patrols, 67% had swimming pools, and between 21% and 45% maintained other types of recreation facilities. Forty-eight percent of associations had attempted to influence local government with respect to police protection, 41% with respect to traffic patterns, 30% with respect to zoning, and 13% with respect to schools.

There is a growing amount of public administration literature on these neighborhood groups. "The benefits of co-production experiments that attack relatively simple problems of service delivery have a good chance to fulfill their objectives."[75] The advantages of this practice include cost sharing, the integration of volunteer and paid workers, and the creation of sources of income for neighborhood associations,[76] in addition to creation of an important form of political participation.[77] Among the potential applications are neighborhood watch patrols; day care; elderly and cultural programs; and alley, street, and small park maintenance.[78] Since associations typically use their own members or private contractors not bound by civil service rules, salaries, and pensions systems, other areas also have been identified as producing potential cost savings, including street cleaning, janitorial services, refuse collection, traffic signal maintenance, asphalt paving, and turf and tree maintenance.[79] These developments have led Nathan Glazer to observe that "the local community or neighborhood now finds itself running services, building houses, managing planning, overseeing a local health center or doing more of these than it used to."[80]

NEIGHBORHOOD LAW ENFORCEMENT

Early law enforcement in the United States had a neighborhood basis. In the early history of large American cities, male citizens were required to stand night watch without pay.[81] A paid constabulary, when created, was frequently appointed by election district.[82] Jefferson's design for ward government contemplated appointment of both a constable and a justice of the peace for each ward.[83]   But these institutions never planted the roots they did in England, reflecting in part the concern repeatedly expressed by Madison concerning

the notorious fractions and oppression which take place in corporate towns limited as the opportunities are, and in little republics when uncontrolled by apprehensions of external danger. Every society will have divisions within it, and in a small society no restraint exists upon the power of a minority to tyrannize over a majority.[84]

These concerns have important implications for both the theory and practice of delegation of law enforcement powers to neighborhood associations. With respect to rule-making powers, a long tradition insists that legislation designed to impose a moral stigma be reserved to the legislature or other body fully representative of the sense of the community at large. While the recent wholesale grant of home rule powers to local governments qualifies this tradition, the courts have remained suspicious of efforts to delegate the formulation of criminal sanctions to entities other than general-purpose governments,[85] and their administrative delegates.

Thus, a proposal for neighborhood government in New York City was careful to suggest that

the legislature could authorize local areas . . . to adopt the bill with lesser but not greater penalties than those specified in the enabling legislation. State restraints on the upper limits of penalties and the definition of offenses would protect those who might be accused of crimes and the uniform nature of the act would facilitate comprehension of a district's laws by police . . . judges . . . travellers and new residents.[86]

It is noted that

[d]elegating some legislative powers to define criminal misdemeanors to a neighborhood government could beneficially reassert the influence of local norms in local "street level" law enforcement. Communities would thereby be empowered to proceed legislatively in choosing the extent to which offenses like prostitution, gambling, homosexuality, drunkenness, loitering, vagrancy and disorderly conduct would be deemed "crimes" subject to prosecution.[87]

Some recent legislation affecting residential community associations moves in this direction. Thus, an Arizona statute permits counties to enact juvenile curfew ordinances for unincorporated areas of the county, providing fines at the petty offense level, "on the request or petition of . . . a homeowners' association which represents a majority of the residents in the area to which the curfew would apply."[88]   A Hawaiian statute provides for notice to condominium associations of alcoholic beverage license applications within a 500-foot radius, and for their denial upon protest by a majority of registered voters within such a radius.[89] A second Arizona statute makes homeowners' associations qualified organizations for purposes of obtaining bingo licenses.[90] A Nevada statute empowers associations to act as corporate entities to "[d]irect the removal of vehicles improperly parked on property owned or leased by the association."[91] While this enactment would appear to give a residential community association only the rights of an ordinary property owner, provisions of this sort are not insignificant, given the widespread municipal legislation restricting the availability of parking to neighborhood residents.[92]

While direct powers to enact penal legislation probably should not, and perhaps cannot, be transferred to residential community associations,[93] these indirect devices--allowing associations to become licensees or objectors, permitting them to apply to the municipality for local legislation, according them the normal rights of citizens or property owners to initiate prosecutions, or permitting them to vary penalties within preset limits--can be used to permit associations a larger measure of control over their social and moral environment, but one that avoids the evils of faction by providing substantial external checks beyond those provided by "exit" and "voice."

Proposals for decentralization of the justice system have borne little fruit. The traditional powers of justices of the peace, notwithstanding Jefferson's urging, owed more to the feudal system than to modern democratic theory, and justices were characteristically appointed rather than elected. "As the law becomes more and more elaborate, and the standard of judicial proof rises, special knowledge is continually becoming more and more necessary for the proper discharge of the duties of a magistrate."[94] On the other hand, as de Tocqueville noted, the lay justice was "not a slave of those legal superstitions which render judges unfit members of a government."[95] The "neighborhood court" proposals of the 1960s were necessarily confined to conciliation processes "for family disputes and some marital issues, such as paternity, support and separation, juvenile delinquencies; landlord-tenant relations; small torts and breaches of contract involving only local residents; and misdemeanors affecting only community members."[96] Contemporary alternative-dispute-resolution proposals generally contemplate procedures tied to the court system. The involvement of residential community associations in this sphere would appear not acceptable as inconsistent with contemporary expectations of individual privacy, save perhaps as to disputes arising from operation and management of the residential property itself.[97]

Finally, there have been proposals for neighborhood operation of probation services, in which "the community representative would assist with personal problems, either associated with the situation that led to the allegation of criminal conduct in the first place or arising from the unprecedented demands of regular employment."[98] Similarly, it has been urged that "[n]uclear and extended families that have successfully raised children in urban areas characterized by a high rate of crime should be used as principal service providers to youngsters with a penchant for delinquency."[99] Similar suggestions have been made with respect to mental health care, one of several areas in which there has been an exploding self-help movement in many nations.[100]

COMMERCIAL ENTERPRISES OF NEIGHBORHOODS

A number of statutes confer proprietary functions on associations. Thus, in addition to the statutes relating to acquisition and operation of recreational facilities previously discussed,[101] Florida also authorized associations to acquire hurricane shutters for their members. The cooperative acquisition of such other commodities as insulation, demand response transportation, tree pruning, energy audits, painting services,and heating oil has been suggested, [102] as has the cooperative operation of food stores[103] and credit unions, and a mundane and obvious but oft-neglected measure--the maintenance of a community bulletin board on each city block.[104] The further reaches of possibilities are catalogued by adherents of the community technology movement and include such proposals as neighborhood skill directories, newspapers,[105] waste disposal, energy production, farming, and fish-raising ventures.[106] More common are community garage sales, bazaars, and the like, which have received special dispensation from some governments.[107]

A number of states in the early 1970s adopted Neighborhood Community Development Acts, which were synthesized by the Advisory Commission for Intergovernmental Relations.[108] These statutes were designed to foster economic development in inner-city neighborhoods[109] but were not notably successful because of such factors as poor industrial sites, inadequate utilities and transportation, high insurance rates, and unskilled labor.[110] They were said to be "good for the psyches of boards of directors of foundations . . . but the multiplier effect of Community Development Corporations is small and their contagion is yet to be proven. . . . [they are] far more complex in their organization and finances than conventional developments in either the private or the public sectors."[111] Most of the statutes are sufficiently widely cast to permit residential community associations to incorporate parallel organizations under them for economic development purposes, thus obtaining the benefits of tax credits for contributions and revenue-bond issuance powers, among other advantages.

NEIGHBORHOOD ELECTION UNITS

Jefferson envisaged his wards as election units.[112] More modern writers have described one effect of the reapportionment decisions as creating "neighborhoods of strangers and jurisdictions without traditions."[113] While the growth of population together with the mechanistic view taken by the Supreme Court would make it difficult to give associations as such separate representatives unless by weighted voting in a small neighborhood council,[114] the size of the typical association corresponds fairly closely to the size of the typical election precinct. There would appear no constitutional or practical objection to the realignment of precinct boundaries to correspond to those of community associations, allowing a common and convenient polling place with poll watchers and election judges drawn from the community.

CONSTITUTIONAL LIMITATIONS AND EXTERNAL RELATIONS

Much has been written as to the degree to which community associations are subject to constitutional constraints.[115] A degree of consensus has begun to emerge in the case law generally holding that they are to be analogized to private associations rather than municipal governments. As an original proposition, this seems a correct evaluation and one that does not have malign effects. Even private associations are subject to the rule of *Shelley v. Kraemer*,[116] which proscribes racial discrimination. The statutory apparatus of federal and state fair housing acts operates to regulate them and prevent invidious forms of religious and other discrimination, while allowing religious organizations, should they choose, to create communities for their members.[117]

The case law[118] makes clear that covenant restrictions are not preempted by local zoning but are superimposed upon it. Of course, they are frequently limited by statute.[119] The restrictions "complement the land use policies of the local units of government and maximize the preferences of the owners of residential units," usually by imposing "detailed aesthetic land use and lifestyle restrictions."[120] For this reason, governments frequently lend aid to enforcement of covenants, either by allowing public authorities to directly enforce them, as in Texas,[121] by requiring building permit applications or zoning appeals to be notified to the affected community association, as in Montgomery [122] and Anne   Arundel Counties[123] in Maryland, by requiring association architectural approval as in Irvine, California, and Marlton, New Jersey,[124] or by providing public mediation and arbitration mechanisms for disputes between associations and their members, as in Montgomery County, Maryland[125] and Florida.[126] California limits the ability of a blocking minority to withhold necessary maintenance,[127] and Florida provides license examinations for community association managers.[128]

Although zoning laws thus far have undergone little amendment to foster community life,[129] a number of the enabling acts for community and condominium regimes expressly prohibit local governments from discriminating against such regimes in their zoning ordinances.[130] The activities of the associations are also constrained in some measure by the common law touch and concern rule (now rapidly being relaxed under the auspices of the Restatement of Servitudes)[131] and by the business judgment rule, construed to protect "expectations of fiscal responsibility and freedom from forced redistributions of wealth compared to citizens of a general purpose government."[132]

The ability of associations to conduct activities going beyond those traditionally associated with property maintenance is also constrained to a small extent by the tax code. In order for an association to be deemed an exempt homeowners' association, at least 85% of all units must be zoned residential, and 60% of income must consist of dues, fees and assessments (as distinct from interest, nonmember and facility payments, and funds received for transportation). Ninety percent of expenses (exclusive of appropriations to reserves) must be for care of association property. However, recreational facilities are considered association property for this purpose.[133] These constraints are minimal since "it may prove more beneficial, tax-wise and economically, for increasing numbers of such homeowners groups to file as regular corporations or unincorporated associations and then to follow a regimen of thorough tax planning, yielding nominal annual tax payments."[134]

A number of statutes are expressly permissive as to activities in which associations may engage.[135] However, to the extent that these activities are not expressly provided for in the original covenants, considerations both of predictability and consent and of fair representation have led to the widespread imposition of supramajority (or majority of all residents) requirements in statutes and bylaws.[136] It would seem critical that in any future development of new powers for community associations, that this model be followed and that acceptance and use of a new power by the association be voluntarily undertaken by a majority of its total membership and be terminable in the same fashion. Any other approach creates the risk that associations will be turned into agents of the state or local government or will be dominated by an activist minority (as with the neighborhood associations established under federal auspices in the 1960s). This is essential to have "public policy utilize mediating structures without destroying them in the process,"[137] and for the groups to be "progressive associations not forming wheels within the wheels of public administration, for that is the only condition on which they won't just become corpses."[138]

Thus, the relationship between community associations and local government should be, in large measure, contractual.

There are some deterrents to greater use of associations to render services. One of these arises from the fact that association dues and assessments are not federally tax deductible.[139] In a number of places, including Pennsbury Village in Allegheny County, Pennsylvania,[140] and Oronque Village in Connecticut,[141] associations have incorporated themselves as municipalities or special service districts to gain the advantage of tax deductibility. This, however, severely limits association ability to renounce the rendition of services, the sorts of restrictions associations may impose, and their voting arrangements unless a parallel, rather than superseding, entity is used to render services. An association that merely renders some governmental-type services by contract with a local or state government avoids assuming the characteristics of a general-purpose government and its property-owners' franchise would therefore not be subject to the restraints of the reapportionment decisions.[142]

There would appear to be no constitutional obstacle preventing federal tax deductibility for all or a portion of community association assessments. In view of the virtually unlimited deductibility of mortgage interest and property taxes, which is illogically coupled with the nontaxation of the imputed rental value of homes, any such dispensation would appear to require curtailment of some of the existing tax benefits. Any deduction for community association charges might be expressly limited to an amount equal to the reduction in property taxes allowed by the local government to association residents. The case for federal creation of such a deduction is exceptionally strong, on grounds of both equity and economy; to the extent that associations perform services that would otherwise be paid for by local taxes, no federal revenue loss would result. Absent federal deductibility, associations would be well advised to seek municipal payment in cash rather than tax abatement in exchange for their rendition of services.

DEVOLUTION OF ZONING POWERS

More recently, a large and growing school of commentators, influenced by the classic article by Professor J. Tiebout,[143] has urged the economic benefits of devolving both zoning powers (particularly the power to lift zoning restrictions) and limited revenue sources and public service provision to local governments. These commentators point out that zoning in many of its aspects amounts to the establishment of a collective property right.[144] "The evolution of suburban land-use controls has effectively transformed the suburban neighborhood into a new form of collectively owned private property."[145]

Entry into communities, if not particular neighborhoods, can frequently be purchased by new uses, either by the payment of exactions or "impact fees" to the local government or by payments to corrupt officers.[146] However, extreme rigidity and resistance to new uses arise in established neighborhoods whose residents are precluded from realizing any direct monetary benefit from their entry. Even where uses, such as convenience stores, day care centers, and accessory apartments, might be welcomed by present residents, fear of exception to established policy makes local governments reluctant to grant permissions. In addition, because the monetary benefit of an isolated use in an established neighborhood is small by comparison with that of a new development in a pristine area, the benefits to the user frequently do not justify his running the gauntlet of an expensive rezoning process.[147]

The ability of existing neighborhoods to adjust to changed demographic patterns has been constrained by zoning, which also has resulted in an imposed uniformity precluding neighborhoods from enriching their character by adding stores and other convenience uses[148] or, conversely, from upgrading their quality through aesthetic protection.[149] Hence, Nelson and others suggest that neighborhood associations be incorporated and authorized to sell entry rights to new uses, either by being accorded authority to impose and waive restrictions (Nelson's scheme) or, alternatively, through a system of nuisance fines.[150]

That relaxation of controls by neighborhood consent speaks to a felt need seems evident. A number of studies suggest that mixed uses such as convenience stores (as distinct from regional shopping centers) actually increase property values in residential neighborhoods.[151] Multifamily units, by contrast, are generally held to have a neutral or negative effect on property values.[152] However, the need for service personnel has caused at least the wealthiest of suburban subdivisions to welcome some developments of this character.[153]

It has been observed that "[t]o the extent local governments can identify in advance the approximate collective gain or loss caused by land use changes, land market performance would be improved if zoning could be bought and sold."[154] The ability of local government to do this is obviously greatest in small subdivisions.

The original Standard Zoning Enabling Act contained a clause allowing 20% of the immediate neighbors of a proposed use to require a three-fourths vote of the local legislative body to secure its approval.[155] While this device was impaired by some Supreme Court opinions of the 1920s,[156] it made explicit what is implicit in any local zoning system. "A community that is thoroughly opposed to a particular project has several brigades to defend its fortress. . . . Thus even though resident homeowners have no vested right to zoning they appear to have reliable political entitlement to the status quo in land use."[157]

Thus, permitting a small collective entity, such as a neighborhood association, to relax zoning restrictions has significant economic advantages. Without such a device "the transaction costs of repurchasing rights held by the community are very high."[158]   With it, necessary adaptations for such things as small, multifamily projects, convenience stores, day care centers, and accessory apartments can be accomplished without resort to the transaction costs attendant on buying out of individual objectors at expensive hearings or the arbitrariness and discrimination attendant upon a system requiring a specified percentage of neighbor consents.[159]

The Supreme Court's objections to the neighbor-consent provisions do not extend to local referendum requirements.[160]   Because these were upheld by analogy to town meetings, a regime that reposed the dispensation power in the literal town meeting of a neighborhood association ought to pass constitutional muster.

Although only limited densification may arise from such consent provisions in the first instance, the ability of homeowner associations to bargain with developers more efficiently than individual landowners and local governments should give rise to an acceleration in the adaptation of established neighborhoods to dramatically changed demographic conditions.   To the extent that this results, there are important agglomeration economies.   "Cities exist because of the advantages of physical proximity. . . . [p]roximity fosters innovation."[161]

The more subtle loss from inefficiently dispersed homes and businesses is the loss of agglomeration economies for firms. . . . Face to face contact is an essential ingredient of most growing businesses. The long term effect of this is a lower standard of living. People will commute more than they should . . . creating more congestion and pollution.[162]

The present ability of a single objector to obstruct and raise the costs of development in an established neighborhood gives rise to resort to "alternative sites . . . in ex-urban and rural communities where the political climate, at least initially, is more favorable to development."[163]

Allowing a dispensing power to neighborhood associations similarly enjoys an acceptability that would not extend to the proposals for outright sale of zoning rights or the neighborhood consent provisions.   "The idea of selling zoning makes us uneasy because [it] breaks down the traditional barriers between public and private"[164]   As Nelson[165] suggests, there would be nothing to preclude the associations from conditioning permission on exactions similar to those now obtained by local government.   Under the new scheme, however, the benefit of the exaction would accrue not to bureaucrats or a diffused citizenry but to those immediately impacted by the new project. "Grant the development neighborhood independence from outside government control over its land use and let the neighborhood decide for itself--through some collective mechanism--how to respond to the pressures of outside market forces."[166] This scheme, it is believed, would enjoy greater support than demands for state-imposed inclusionary zoning. "The aim in existing neighborhoods is to increase and perfect the rights of the neighborhood residents who are presently there. These residents thus represent a covenanted constituency with a strong direct influence in the outcome--a formula for maximum political influence in the American system."[167]

HISTORIC AND SPECIAL DISTRICT POWERS

In addition to providing neighborhoods with a dispensing power, there is also an economic case for allowing them to impose restrictions, such as aesthetic restrictions, which do not impose significant externalities. Thus, Nelson urges "a lenient attitude toward the creation of historic and other special districts in neighborhoods, going along with the subterfuges involved in many claims to historic significance."[168] Many states allow the establishment of historic districts by less-than-unanimous consent, and a recent monograph describes the broadening of the "historic district" concept to include a multitude of "special districts."[169] The authors of this study suggest that procedural and substantive standards for creation of such special districts be written into state law, so as to provide protection for dissenting residents and to guard against externalities.[170]

A similar, more sympathetic appeal for enabling legislation urges that states are "the captives of local government lobbies that do not want the competition of formally-constituted neighborhoods. . . . [o]ne step is to create through state constitutions or enabling acts a broad range of political and governmental opportunities so that citizens have the ability to choose between alternative modes of governance."[171] It is suggested that such neighborhood associations or municipal service districts be allocated a percentage of property taxes. A similar emphasis on competition between governmental units informed proposals for neighborhood service districts in New York City.[172] More generally, it has been noted that "[t]he small unit of government serves as an effective check on tendencies to interfere with private choices. . . . [P]lanning in the United States does not yet seem too conscious of the possibility that the price mechanism is a more adaptable and flexible method of land use allocation than a flexible plan administered by an inflexible administrator."[173]

THE FUTURE OF NEIGHBORHOOD

Resistance to this viewpoint lays stress on the proposition that "privatization has the consequence of segregating the population according to income, social status, social values and other personal characteristics that define the character of a neighborhood. . . . Barriers and social divisions among the residents of a metropolitan area may be raised rather than lowered."[174] Against this, there are a number of things to be said. Even the greatest postwar sociologist of the Left, C. Wright Mills, observed: "The members of masses in a metropolitan society know one another only as fractions in a specialized milieu. Prejudgment and stereotype flourish when people meet in such ways. The human reality of others does not, cannot, come through."[175]

It is no accident that New York, the most anonymous of American cities, has some of the worst race relations. The barriers referred to already exist, as a result of government zoning action and the balkanization of metropolitan areas, and community associations can do little to reinforce them. On the contrary, in a nation in which the dollar has been, over time, a universal solvent, transferring powers to a small market-sensitive entity may give rise, in time, to a breakdown of restrictions. Certainly, nothing else has worked. "Allowing greater leeway for market transactions in land may be the only way that those currently excluded--such as inner city residents--will be able to break through the walls of suburban exclusion."[176]

The aspiration for economically mixed residential units has in any case been questioned by many writers, beginning with Rousseau, who saw equality and relative homogeneity as necessary to direct democracy. Thus Peter Mann,[177] in criticizing schemes for "socially balanced" neighborhood units, has urged "Let us begin to think again from a sociological rather than an ideological basis:" while Peter Wolf has noted that "the fascinating history of fantasy, illusion and utopianism throughout the history of architecture and urbanism exists principally because important ideas were released without any notion of how they might be achieved."[178] To these observers the problems of the cities are social more than economic: [t]he problem of the city is no longer functional organization-- the fitting together of places for work, residence, recreation, and the circulation systems that connect them--but instead is the issue of human association--finding the patterns that will enable people to live together."[179] Robert Putnam observed on the need for building social capital:

[n]etworks of civic engagement improve the flow of information about the trustworthiness of individuals, embody past success at collaboration . . . increase the potential costs to a defector . . . foster robust norms of reciprocity . . . In the absence of trust, there can be no certainty in contracts and hence no force to the laws, and a society in that

condition is effectively reduced to a state of semi-savagery . . . the savages who will only give with the right hand if they simultaneously receive with the left.[180]

The paramount need of the inner city is for the development of such "networks of civic engagement", and we may recall Lewis Mumford's observation that "most of the fresh initiatives in urban design . . . were first tried out in the suburb."[181]   The residential association is no exception to this rule.   The task for Americans would appear to lie in the replication on city streets or blocks of the neighborhood associations of the suburbs--not in rejecting their role in the jurisdictions of their origin.   In rejecting the ideal and possibility of a socially balanced neighborhood unit, Richard Dewey pertinently observed:

If the [neighborhood] principle proves to be of prime importance in making our cities more liveable, if it be the means of bringing more democratic control to the city as Cooley warned must be done . . . it will be because of its cautious application in accord with the best available knowledge of man's behavior in an urban environment.[182]

As noted by Page Smith, "we have today with the breakdown of the power of the local community a few national orthodoxies rather than many parochial ones . . . [that] permitted the dissenter to form, with his fellows, his own community of conformity."[183]

NOTES

1. J. Bryce, *The American Commonwealth* (1895), vol. 1, at 637.

2. P. Smith, *As a City upon a Hill: The Town In American History* (1968), at 11, 13.

3. L. Mumford, *The City in History* (1961), at 179.

4. Mumford, *supra* note 3, at 331.

5. *Id*

6. Emerson, *Journals* (1857), quoted in Mumford, *supra* note 3, at 333; Bureau of the Census, *1982 Census of Governments* (1983), at 105, 237, 241, 254, 281, 303, 333. See also T. Cooley, *Constitutional Limitations* (8th ed. 1927), at 236; (3d ed. 1874), at 129. See J. Mansbridge, *Beyond Adversary Democracy* (1980).

7. R. Briffault, *Our Localism*, 90 Columbia Law Review 1, 74 n.314 (1990), citing the 1982 U.S. Census of Governments.

8. H. G. Wells, *Mankind in the Making* (1903) in *Area and Power* (A. Maass ed. 1959), at 217.

9. Hunt v. City of Pittsburgh (1907). See the lamentations of J. Frug, *The City as a Legal Concept*, 93 Harvard Law Review 4 (1979); of F. Michelman, *Law's Republic*, 97 Yale Law Journal 1493 (1988); and of J. Hartog, *Public Property and Private Power: The Corporation of the City of New York in American Law, 1730-1870* (1983). On the weakness of town government, see M. Gottdiener, *Planned Sprawl* (1977).

10. J. Dillon, *Treatise on the Law of Municipal Corporations* (1872), 101-2. For a defense of the rule on the basis that it limits economically damaging externalities, see C. Gillette, *In Partial Praise of Dillon's Rule*, 67 Chi-Kent Law Review 959 (1991).

11. J. Rousseau, *Social Contract*, ch. IV. On restrictive annexation laws, see G. Liner, *Institutional Constraints and Annexation Activity in the U.S.*, 30 Urban Studies 1371 (1993).

12. *Id.*

13. W. Farr et al., *Decentralizing City Government: A Practical Study of a Radical Proposal for New York City* (1972), at 43, see also D. Moynihan, *Maximum Feasible Misunderstanding: Community Action in the War on Poverty* (1969).

14. I. Kristol, *Decentralization for What?* 11 Public Interest (1968), at 9-20; see P. Berger and R. Neuhaus, *To Empower People* (1977), at 40.

15. D. Yates, *Neighborhood Democracy* (1973), at 159.

16. C. Lindblom, *Concepts of Community* (1968), at 17.

17. L. Mumford, *supra* note 3, at 422-23.

18. S. Warner, *The Urban Wilderness* (1972), at 21.

19. L. Mumford, *The Neighborhood and the Neighborhood Unit*, 24 Town Planning Review 256, 257 (1954).

20. Hartog, *supra* note 9, at 168.

21. S. Diamond, *Death and Transfiguration of Benefit Taxation*, 12 Journal Legal Studies 201 (1983). See D. Hagman and Miscynski, *Windfalls for Wipeouts* (1978), at 311-35, 612-14.

22. C. Weller, *NeglectedNeighborhoods: Stories of Life in the Alleys, Tenements and Shanties of the Nation's Capital* (1909), at 144-21.

23. *Id.* at 122.

24. D. Hayden, *Redesigning The American Dream: The Future of Housing, Work and Family Life* (1984), at 179.

25. Weller, *supra* note 22, at 122.

26. A. Moudon, *Introduction* in *Public Streets for Public Use* (A. Moudon ed. 1987), at i.

27. B. Ryan, *Street Vacations*, in *Public Streets for Public Use* (A. Moudon ed. 1987), at 284-85.

28. *Id.*

29. *Id.* at 285. On Chicago, see New York Times, January 23, 1993, sec. I., at pg. 6. On the benefits of cul-de-sacs, see R. Taylor, *Block Crime and Fear*, 21 Journal of Research in Crime and Delinquency 303 (1984); B. Brown, *Social Cohesiveness and Territoriality: The Influence of Cul-de-sacs*, 17 Environment and Behavior 539 (1985).

30. The St. Louis County associations have generated a substantial literature. See O. Newman, *Communities of Interest* (1972), at 124-56, R. Oakerson, *Private Street Associations in St. Louis*, in U.S. Advisory Commission on Intergovernmental Relations, *Residential Community Associations: Private Governments in the Intergovernmental System* (1989) (hereafter "ACIR-RCA"), at 55-62; ACIR, *MetropolitanOrganization: The St. Louis Case* (1988); Beito, *The Private Places of St. Louis, 1869-1920* (1988); R. Vickery, *Anthrophysical Form: Two Families and their Neighborhood Environments* (1972).

31. D. Appleyard, *Liveable Streets* (1981), at 313.

32. See Newman, *supra* note 30 at 128; Oakerson, *supra* note 30, at 55. Tax rebate programs also exist in Houston and Kansas City; see ACIR-RCA, at 20. And in Montgomery County, Maryland, with respect to collector roads in private subdivisions that never were under public ownership; see Montgomery County Code, sec. 24B, 14-19.

33. See City of St. Louis Charter, art I. sec. 14 and art. XXI sec. 14 (1978); Note, *The Law and Private Streets*, 5 St. Louis University Law Journal 588 (1954).

34. Newman, *supra* note 30, at 155. It may be doubted that this sort of rule making by local option presents constitutional difficulties, at least where the ultimate decision is subject to review by a court or local public body. See G. Liebmann, *Delegation to Private Parties in American Constitutional Law*, 50 Indiana Law Journal 650, 671-72 (1975). See Browning v. Hooper, 269 U.S. 396 (1926) (creation of special districts on approval by a court); U.S. v. Rock Royal Cooperative, 307 U.S. 533 (1939) (creation of private association with price control powers on approval of an administrator).

35. A. Moudon and Untermann, *Grids Revisited,* in *Public Streets for Public Use* (A. Moudon ed. 1987), at 148.

36. W. Crouch and McHenry, Los Angeles, in *Great Cities* (W. Robson ed. 2d ed. 1957), at 319. A similar suggestion for "direct participation of street users in the design and management of streets" is made in M. Franks, *The Making of Democratic Streets,* in Moudon, *Public Streets for Public Use* (A. Moudon ed. 1987), at 29.

37. P. Wolf, *Rethinking the Urban Street: Its Economic Context,* in *On Streets* (S. Anderson ed. 1978), at 380-82.

38. C. Rose, *The Comedy of the Commons*, 53 University of Chicago Law Review 211, 781 (1986).

39. J. Cunningham, *The Resurgent Neighborhood* (1965).

40. N.Y. Exec. Law sec. 848.

41. Indiana Code sec. 14.6.35.

42. Fla. Stat. Ann. secs. 718.111(8), 718.111(13)(d), 718.114 (1992).

43. L. Taylor, *Urban Open Space* (1979); R. Hester, *Neighborhood Space* (1985); Trust for Public Land, *Neighborhood Land Revitalization Manual* (1981); K. Lynch, *A Theory of Good City Form* (1981); M. Frazer and P. Ferrera, *Sourcebook on Enterprise Zones* (1981), ch. 5; Cohen, *Neighborhood Planning and Political Capacity Building*, 19 Urban Affairs Quarterly 333 (1984).

44. U.S. Advisory Commission on Intergovernmental Relations, 2 *Fiscal Balance in the American Federal System* (1962), at 16-17; ACIR, *Model State Legislation: Neighborhood Subunits of Government, 1970 Cumulative ACIR State Legislative Program* (1969).

45. See S. Rothman, *Woman's Proper Place* (1978), at 271.

46. Child Care and Development Block Grant Act of 1990, 42 U.S.C.A. sec. 9858a-p.

47. A. Cohen, *Zoning for Family Day Care*, in *Zoning and Planning Law Handbook* (K. Young ed. 1991), at 105, 115-33. Former Secretary of Health, Education and Welfare Elliott Richardson urged in 1976 that "day care centers can be influenced to locate by zoning by-laws which reflect the overall community plan." From E. Richardson, *The Creative Balance* (1976), at 294.

In spite of adverse court decisions in Indiana and California (where there is conflicting case law), the validity under federal legislation of such legislation seems clear. See Keystone Bituminous Coal Assn. v. De Benedictis, 480 U.S. 470, 503 (1987); E. Ziegler, *State Abrogation of Private Covenants*, in *1991 Zoning and Planning Handbook* (K. Young ed. 1991), at 221.

48. American Law Institute, *Restatement of Servitudes*, Council Draft no. 4, sec. 4.3, at 309-10.

49. Md. Real Prop. Code Ann. sec. 11B-101, enacted by ch. 321 of the Acts of 1987.

50. See J. Steiner, *Community Organization* (1925), at 239-53; C. Dinwiddie, *Community Responsibility* (1918); W. Phillips, *Adventuring for Democracy* (1940); S. Eldridge, *Community Organization and Citizenship*, 7 Social Forces 140 (1923); S. Lowrie, *The Social Unit An Experiment in Politics*, 9 National Municipal Review (1923), at 553-66; M. Follett, *The New State* (1934).

51. Rothman, supra note 45; Bakelhamer et al., *Child Health Policy: A Review of Federal Involvement*, 29 Advances in Pediatrics 211 (1982); B. Stokes, *Local Responses to Global Problems* (1978), at 29-40; L. Levin, *Self-Care, An International Perspective, Social Policy* (1976).

52. See 2 *Writings of Thomas Jefferson* (Ford ed.), at 220-37; A. Koch and W. Piden, *The Life and Selected Writings of Thomas Jefferson* (1944), at 661-62; R. Honeywell, *The Educational Work of Thomas Jefferson*, ch. 2, app. (1931).

53. U.S. Bureau of Education, *Proposed Community Forum Bill* (1922); E. Glueck, *Community Use of Schools* (1927); C. Perry, *Extension of Public Education* (1915); Steiner, *supra* note 50 (1925), at 136-51; E. White, *Community Centers in School Buildings*, 1923 National Conference on Social Work (1923), at 440-44.

54. L. Mumford, *supra* note 19.

55. P. Berger, *Facing Up to Modernity* (1977), at 139.

56. B. Barber, *Strong Democracy* (1984), at 146 n.8.

57. 20 U.S.C.A. sec. 1701(a). See also sec. 1705 ("assignment to the school nearest his residence"); and sec. 1714 ("closest or most closest to his place of residence").

58. Equal Access Act of 1984, 20 U.S.C.A. sec. 4071 (1984), upheld against establishment clause challenge in Board of Education v. Mergens, 496 U.S. 226 (1990).

59. See C. Faher, *Is Local Control of Schools Still a Viable Option?*, 14 Harvard Journal of Law and Public Policy 447, 467-72 (1991); R. Zerchykov et al., *State Mandates for School Advisory Councils* (1980); Ky. Rev. Stat. secs. 160.155, 160.345 (Baldwin Supp. 1990); Cal. Educ. Code. secs. 52000-52038, 52850-52870 (West 1991).

60. See M. Peck, *Independent Special Districts* (1962); Willoughby, *The Quiet Alliance*, 39 Southern California Law Review 72 (1965). In Browning v. Hooper, 26 U.S. 396, 405-066 (1926), the Supreme Court declared: "[I]t is essential to due process of law that . . . owners be given notice and opportunity to be heard where . . . the district was not created by the legislature and there has been no legislative determination that their property will be benefitted by the local improvement."

61. R. Nelson, *Zoning Myth and Practice*, in *Zoning and the American Dream* (C. Haar et al. eds. 1989), at 312; see also W. Fischel, *The Economics of Zoning Laws* (1985), at 331; R. Nelson, *Private Neighborhoods*, in *Land Reform: American Style*, (C. Geisler et al. eds. 1984), at 319-37; C. Rose, *Preservation and Community*, 33 Stanford Law Review 473 (1981).

62. Note, *Historic Districts: Preserving City Neighborhoods for the Privileged*, 60 New York University Law Review 64 (1985). The best discussion of the "historic district" phenomenon remains Rose, *supra* note 61.

63. See R. Babcock et al., *Special Districts: The Ultimate in Neighborhood Zoning* (1990). For authorization of creation of such districts by Maryland municipalities other than Baltimore City, see Md. Code, art. 23A, secs. 2(b)35, 44, 44A (1990 Repl. Vol.).

64. See [British] Law Commission, Law of Positive and Restrictive Covenants.

65. See H. Dyson, *French Real Property and Succession Law* (2d ed. 1991), at 87.

66. See Note, *Affirmative Duties Running with the Land*, 35 New York University Law Review 734 (1960); 2 *American Law of Contracts* (A. Casner, ed. 1952), sec. 9.24; J. Winokur, *Association Administered Servitude Regimes*, in ACIR-RCA, *supra* note 30, at 85, 89 n.9.

67. On the early history, see P. Rohan, *Real Estate Transactions: Home Owner Associations and PUDs* (1988), sec. 2.02.

68. See R. Isaac, *The Neighborhood Theory: An Analysis of Its Adequacy*, 14 Journal of American Planning Association 15 (1948).

69. Urban Land Institute, *Community Builders' Handbook* (1950); National Association of Home Builders, *Home Builders' Manual for Land Development* (1950). See C. Woodbury, *Housing in the Redevelopment of American Cities*, 25 Land Economics 397 (1949); S. Dillick, *Community Organization for Neighborhood Development* (1953); S. Rasmussen, *Neighborhood Planning*, 27 Town Planning Review 197 (1957).

70. Federal Housing Association, *Planned Unit Development with a Homes Association* (1963).

71. ACIR-RCA, *supra* note 30, at 1, 3, 27; R. Louv, *America II* (1983), at 109-10.

72. ACIR-RCA, *supra* note 30, at 4, 11, 12, 21.

73. R. Wood, *Suburbia: Its People and their Politics* (1958), at 16-17.

74. S. Dillick, *supra* note 69, at 119.

75. D. Yates, *supra* note 15, at 123.

76. M. Kotler, *Neighborhood Delivery of Environmental Services* (1983).

77. G. Whitaker, *Co-Production: Citizen Participation in Service Delivery*, 40 Public Administration Review 240, 244 (1980).

78. W. Colman, *State and Local Government and Public-Private Partnerships* (1989), at 156.

79. *Id.*

80. For other discussions of coproduction see Suskind and Elliott, *Paternalism, Conflict and Co-Production: Learning from Citizen Action and Citizen Participation in Western Europe* (1983); Koven, *Coproduction of Law Enforcement Services*, 27 Urban Affairs Quarterly 457 (1992); C. Levine, *Citizenship and Service Delivery*, 44 Public Administration Review 78 (1984); J. Brudney and R. England, *Toward a Definition of the Co-Production Concept*, 43 Public Administration Review 59 (1983); G. Frederickson, *Recovery of Civism in Public Administration*, 41 Public Administration Review 501 (1981); J. Ferris, *Co-Provision, Citizen Time and Money Donations in Public Service Provision*, 44 Public Administration Review 324 (1984); R. Yin, *Citizen Organizations: Increasing Client Control over Services* (1973). "RCAs account for the most significant privatization of local government responsibilities in recent times." From ACIR-RCA, *supra* note 30, at 18.

81. H. Locke, *The Evolution of Contemporary Police Services* in Garmine, *Local Government Police Management* (1977). See E. Monkkonen, *Police in Urban America, 1860-1920* (1981).

82. See H. Adams, *Norman Constables in America* (1883).

83. See S. Huntington, *The Founding Fathers and the Division of Powers*, in *Area and Power*, (A. Maass ed., 1959), at 177.

84. Letter from Madison to Jefferson, October 24, 1787, in J. Madison, 5 *Works*, at 28-29. See also The Federalist no. 10, at 58-62; no. 14, at 80; no. 43, at 84; no. 51, at 339-41 (Modern Library ed.). See Huntington, *supra* note 83. New England town meetings have elaborate procedural rules to guard against factional excesses, including "executive budget" systems.

85. See Olinger v. People, 344 P.2d 689 (Colo. 1959)(voters of conservancy districts); People v. Malmud, 158 N.Y.S.2d 838, *revd. on other grounds*, 4 App. Div. 2d 86, 164 N.Y.S. 2d 204 (N.Y. App. Div. 1957)(bondholders of bridge and tunnel authority). There was an early suspicion, since overcome, of delegations of power to enact criminal legislation to public administrative agencies. See United States v. Grimaud, 220 U.S. 506 (1911). Compare Mistretta v. United States, 488 U.S. 361 (1989).

86. See W. Farr et al., *supra* note 13, at 108-09, and the fuller elaboration in R. Danzig, *Toward the Creation of a Complementary Decentralized System of Criminal Justice*, 26 Stanford Law Review 1, 18 (1973).

87. Farr et al., *supra* note 13, at 108.

88. Ariz. Rev. Stat. Ann. sec. 11-251(40).

89. Haw. Rev. Stat. sec. 281(57-59). It is disputed whether residential community associations may prohibit alcoholic beverage consumption within their common areas. See Hidden Harbor Estate v. Norman, 309 So.2d 180 (Fla. Dist. Ct. App. 1975).

90. Ariz. Rev. Stat. Ann. secs. 5-401(10) and 5-401(25)(1992).

91. Nev. Rev. Stat. sec. 116.3102(g), part of the state's common interest ownership act. Similar arrangements preval with respect to animal control in Montgomery County, Maryland, and parking and traffic restrictions on RCA property in Fairfax County, Virginia. See ACIR-RCA, *supra* note 30, at 19.

92. The validity of such restrictions was upheld in County Bd. of Arlington v. Richards, 434 U.S. 5 (1977)("the Equal Protection Clause does not presume distinctions between residents and nonresidents of a local neighborhood to be invidious").

93. But see Fla. Stat. Ann. sec. 718,393(d)(3) (1992)(conferring on community associations power to fine residents up to $50 for violation of association rules).

94. J. Stephen, *History of the Criminal Law of England* (1883), at 299.

95. A. de Tocqueville, 1 *Democracy in America* (Vintage ed. 1954), at 77.

96. W. Farr et al., *supra* note 8, at 115.

97. See Israel Land Law sec. 72-77 (1969). Even such devotees of neighborhood power as D. Morris and K. Hess, *Neighborhood Power: The New Localism* (1975), at 110, refer to neighborhood courts as "open to petty jealousies and personal rivalries."

98. Farr et al., *supra* note 13, at 116.

99. R. Woodstek, *A Summons to Life* (1981), at 131.

100. A. Naperstek, *Neighborhood Networks for Humane Mental Health Care* (1982). For an interesting survey of self-help movements, see D.Pancoast et al., *Rediscovering Self Help: Its Role in Social Care* (1983), for British statutes, including extensive bibliographies, see R. Adams, *Self-Help, Social Work and Empowerment* (1990); B. Knight, *Self-Help in the Inner City* (1981). See also Symposium, *Self-Help, Voluntarism, and Citizen Participation in Comparative Perspective*, 15 Journal of Volunteer Action Research, no.2, (1986), at 3-90.

101. Fla. Stat. Ann. sec. 718.113(5) (1992).

102. H. Hallman, *Neighborhoods, Their Place in Urban Life* (1984), at 167.

103. See Morris and Hess, *supra* note 97 at 77.

104. *Id.* Credit unions may now be established by "groups within a well-defined neighborhood, community, or rural district." 12 U.S.C.A. sec. 1759. See B. Caftel, *Community Development Credit Unions* (1978).

105. See D. Popenoe, *Private Pleasure, Public Plight* (1991), at 157, citing M. Janowitz, *The Community Press in an Urban Setting* (1952) ("Probably the most important single vehicle for the advancement of community political and social autonomy is a local newspaper."). Local broadsheets played a major role in eighteenth-century law enforcement. Lord Mansfield declared in 1783: "How are felons in general taken up? From descriptions of them circulated in handbills." On the unjustified and fortuitous demise of this device, see J. Styles, *Print and Policing*, in *Policing and Prosection in England, 1750-1850* (D. Hay and F. Snyder eds., 1989), at 56. "Taxation policies, postal

regulations and other factors should be reexamined with a view toward sustaining neighborhood newspapers." From Berger and Neuhaus, *supra* note 51.

106. K. Hess, *Community Technology* (1979); Stokes, *supra* note 51.

107. See, for example, Anne Arundel County (Md.) Code sec. 6-7-301 (exemption from admission and amusement taxes for residential community association activities).

108. Advisory Commission on Intergovernmental Relations, *Neighborhood Improvement Assistance and Organization Act* (1984). Typical of the statutes is that of Wisconsin, Wis. Stat. Ann. sec. 234,94 *et seq.*, which provides for incorporation of community development corporations with specific geographic boundaries. Such corporations must permit all resident adults to belong, on payment of a fee not exceeding $10. See also Cal. Gov't Code sec. 533.11 (West 1983) (Mello-Roos Community Facilities Act of 1982).

109. See Comment, *Community Development Corporations*, 83 Harvard Law Review 1558 (1970).

110. T. Zimmerman, *The Federated City: Community Control in Large Cities* (1972), at 26 (the statutes were enacted in Florida, Iowa, Michigan, Minnesota, and New York).

111. Editorial, Wall Street Journal, 10 December 1986, quoted in D. Harloe, New *Ideas for Housing. The Experience of Three Countries* (1990), at 92.

112. Huntington, *supra* note 83.

113. R. Hanson, *The Political Thicket: Reapportionment and Constitutional Democracy* (1966), at 132.

114. See M. Kotler, *Neighborhood Government: The Local Foundation of Political Life* (1969) (urging that "neighborhoods . . . ally themselves to devise city constitutions that distribute power among the neighborhoods and federate that power in a common city government").

115. In support of this view, see R. Epstein, *Covenants and Constitutions*, 73 Cornell Law Review 906 (1988); U. Reichman, *Residential Private Governments*, 43 University Chicago Law Review 253 (1976); R. Ellickson, *Alternatives to Zoning*, 40 University Chicago Law Review 681 (1973); White Egret Condominium v. Franklin, 379 So.2d. 346 (Fla. 1980) (upholding age restriction); Green v. Greenbelt Homes, 194 A.2d. 273 (Md. 1963) (upholding prohibition on cohabitation by unrelated persons). But see Taormina Theosophical Community v. Silver, 190 Cal. Rptr. 38 (Cal. Ct. App. 1983)(limiting residence to theosophical society members unenforceable); State v. Celmer, 404 A.2d 1 (N.J. 1979)(same as to camp meeting members). See Note, The Rule of Law in

Residential Associations, 99 Harvard Law Review 472 (1985); Note, Judicial Review of Condominium Rulemaking, 94 Harvard Law Review 647 (1981).

116. 334 U.S. 1 (1948).

117. See SMI Industries v. Lanard & Axilbund, 481 F. Supp. 459 (E.D.Pa. 1979); Stephanus v. Anderson, 613 P.2d. 533, 540-41 (Wash. 1980). But see the cases cited *supra* note 115. "[T]he religious experience often cannot be separated from the fate of a community--that it may bind the present with the past and the future and play an important role in shaping the character of its members." From M. Glendon and R. Yanes, *Structural Free Exercise*, 90 Michigan Law Review 477, 506 (1991). "Whether judicial enforcement of servitudes other than racial restrictions involves sufficient state action to subject the servitude to limits imposed by the Fourteenth Amendment has generally been doubted, but has not been definitively decided." From Restatement (Third) of Servitudes sec. 3.1, cmt. f.

118. Omega Corp. v. Mallory, 319 S.E. 2d 728 (Va. 1984); Annison v. Hoover, 517 So. 2d 420 (La.Ct.App. 1987); Schwartz v. State, 408 N.Y.S.2d 239 (N.Y. Ct. Cl. 1978); Harwick v. Indian Creek Country Club, 142 So.2d 128 (Fla. App. 1962). See R. Tarlock, *Residential Community Associations and Land Use Controls*, in ACIR-RCA, *supra* at 75, 81.

119. See Park Redlands Control Comm. v. Simon, 226 Cal. Rep. 199 (Cal. Ct. App. 1986)(civil rights law applied to age restrictions); 42 U.S.C.A. sec. 3601ff. (prohibiting age restrictions except as to retirement communities); Crane Neck Ass'n v. New York Community Group, 472 N.Y.S.2d. 901 (N.Y. 1984) (statutes promoting deinstitutionalization). See generally E. Ziegler, *supra* note 47, at 125-39.

120. Tarlock, *supra*, note 118.

121. See B. Siegan, *Land Use Without Zoning* (1972); Vernon's Texas Code Ann. Property sec. 203.003. also secs. 201.001, 201.009 (procedure for extending life of covenants on petition of 75% of owners except as to owners expressly opting out).

122. Montgomery County (Md.) Code sec. 8-24 (building permits).

123. Anne Arundel County (Md.) Code sec. 3-2-103 (zoning appeals).

124. ACIR-RCA, *supra* note 30, at 19.

125. *Id.* at 19.

126. Fla. Stat. Ann. sec. 718, 111(19) (1992).

127. S. Barton and C. Silverman, *The Political Life of Mandatory Homeowners'*
Associations(1989), at 36. California also allows RCAs to obtain court authorization for
amendments to association documents. ACIR-RCA, *supra* note 30, at 20.

128. Fla. Stat. Ann. sec. 468,431 (1992) (the statute applies only to managers who
offer their services "for remuneration and for the public.") In addition, as previously
noted, some states have expanded the immunities of community associations.

129. The starts in this direction are summarized in G. Liebmann, Suburban Zoning:
Two Modest Proposals, 25 Real Property, Prob. & Trust Journal 1 (1991).

130. "Neither shall any condominium be treated differently by any zoning or other
land use ordinance which would permit a physically identical project or development
under a different form of ownership." Va. Stat. 55.79.43A. See also Report of the
Maryland Governor's Commission on Condominiums, Cooperatives and Homeowners'
Associations, January 27, 1986; Oregon Administrative Reporter 660-07-022.

131. See Restatement (Third) of Servitudes sec. 3.2, superseding Restatement of
Property, Landlord and Tenant, ch. 16.

132. Tarlock, *supra* note 118, at 75, 79.

133. 26 U.S.C. sec. 528. See Federal Register 1,528; Revenue Rulings 74-17, 74-1
CB 130; 74-99, 74-1 CB 131; W. Hyatt, *Community Association Law* (2d.ed. 1988), at
6.03.

134. D. Campbell-Hall, *Homeowners Associations-Is Tax Exemption Worth the*
Effort? 20 Real Property, Probate & Trust Journal 647, 662 (1985).

135. See Maryland Report, *supra* note 130; Fla. Stat. Ann. sec. 718, 112(3)(c)(1992);
Va Code Ann. 55-79.80(c) (1992) ("shall not be construed to prohibit the grant, by the
condominium instruments of other powers and responsibilities").

136. See, for example, Md. Real Prop. Code Ann., art. llB 111 (majority of all
residents not of quorum, needed to limit family day care). For proposals that would allow
a supermajority of residents to relax deed restrictions (a provision included in many
restrictions themselves), see R. Oakerson, *Residential Community Associations: Further*
Differentiating the Organization of Local Public Economies, in ACIR-RCA, *supra* note
30, at 105, 108.

137. Berger, *supra* note 55, at 139-40.

138. S. Weil, *The Need For Roots* (1944), at 166. There is scope, however, for the sort of training of neighborhood counselors proposed by E. Richardson, *Significant Individual Participation: The New Challenge in American Government*, 15 University Chicago Law School Record No. 2 (1967), at 42. Similar British proposals for community development officers were made in the Skeffington Report on Public Participation in Planning but were not accepted by the government. See N. Taylor, *The Village in the City* (1973), at 220.

139. As noted above, a number of states allow tax credits for payments to neighborhood associations or accord association residents a credit against property taxes representing the cost of services rendered by the association: see note 128.

140. See U.S. Advisory Commission on Intergovernmental Relations, *Metropolitan Organization: The Allegheny County Case* (1989).

141. ACIR-RCA, *supra* note 30, at 19.

142. See Ball v. James, 451 U.S. 355 (1981); Salyer Land Co. v. Tulare Lake Basin Water Storage Dist., 410 U.S. 719 (1973). Cf. W. Rehnquist, *The Adversary Society*, 33 University of Miami Law Review 11 (1978)(quoted in Glendon, *Structural Free Exercise*, 90 Michigan Law Review 477, 537 (1991)(those who make our laws . . . serve us poorly if they do not recognize that the world in which we live is an intricate web of relationships between people, private institutions and government at is various levels"). Nelson pertinently inquires: "Could there be different types of voting rights, varying with the issue under consideration?" See Nelson, *The Privatization of Local Government: From Zoning To RCA's*, in ACIR-RCA, *supra* note 30, at 45, 51.

143. J. Tiebout, *A Pure Theory of Local Expenditures*, 64 Journal of Political Economy 416 (1956).

144. This theme has been frequently reiterated in the work of Robert H. Nelson. See R. Nelson, *Marketable Zoning*, Land Use Law & Zoning Digest (1985).

145. R. Nelson, in Geisler and Popper, *supra* note 61, at 319.

146. *Id.* at 329. See also W. Fischel, *Introduction*, 66 Land Economics (1990), at 229-30 (citing D. Eppler et al., *Community Development with Endogenous Land Use Controls*, 35 Journal of Public Economics 133 (1988), and J. Henderson, *Community Development: The Effects of Growth and Uncertainty*, 70 American Economic Review 894 (1980)("Devices such as development exactions, contract zoning and impact fees are ad hoc techniques that partly integrate community revenue with land use controls"). See also W. Fischel, *Do Growth Controls Matter?* (1990), at 41; R. Babcock, *Exactions*, 50 Law & Contemporary Problems 1 (1987). The failure to reassess older properties has also

been described as a way of charging developers marginal costs. See Fischel, *supra* note 61, at 331.

147. See G. Liebmann, *The Modernization of Zoning: Enabling Act Revision as a Means to Reform*, 23 Urban Lawyer 1, 2 (1991).

148. F. Freund, *Some Inadequately Discussed Problems of the Law of Zoning*, in *Planning Problems of Town, City and Region* (1929), at 93.

149. On aesthetic zoning, see for example, Mayor and Council v. Mano Swartz, 299 A.2d 828 (1973)(aesthetic controls proscribed but controls to protect established values permitted). G. Liebmann, *Maryland Zoning: The Court and Its Critics*, 27 Maryland Law Review 39 (1965).

150. See Ellickson, *supra* note 115.

151. W. Stull, *Community Environment, Zoning, and the Market Value of Single Family Homes*, 18 Journal of Law and Economics 535 (1975). A similar conclusion (except as to homes immediately abutting the commercial use) was reached in Siegan, *supra* note 121, a study of the land-use regime in Houston, a city without zoning controls. On the case for convenience stores in residential neighborhoods, see Liebmann, *supra* note 129; see also Nelson, *Private Neighborhoods*, *supra* note 61, at 330.

152. Various studies are cited in A. Tarlock, *Residential Community Associations and Land Use Controls*, in ACIR-RCA, *supra* note 30, at 75, 90 n.16.

153. See R. Ellickson, *The Irony of Inclusionary Zoning*, 54 Southern California Law Review 1167 (1981).

154. D. Mills, *Zoning Rights and Land Development Timing*, *supra* note 61; see also D. Kmiec, Deregulating Land Use, 130 Univeristy of Pennsylvania Law Review 28 (1981).

155. See the discussion in W. Fischel, *supra* note 61. The provision of the SZEA (State Zoning Enabling Act) was sec. 5; see American Law Institute, Model Land Development Code, Tent. Dr. no. 1, app. A, at 210, 216-17 (1968).

156. McBain, *Law Making by Property Owners*, 36 Political Science Quarterly 617 (1921); Liebmann, supra note 34, at 675-80.

157. Fischel, *supra* note 61, at 36. See G. Lefcoe, *Land Development in Crowded Places: Lessons from Abroad* (1979), at 11-38, 149-51. Fischel also notes that there is little danger that already established neighborhoods will be menaced by new low-income

housing projects, at least where public subsidy is absent, since only small projects not enjoying economies of scale are possible in already-established neighborhoods.

158. Fischel, *Do Growth Controls Matter? supra* note 146, at 21 ("Zoning tends to become a rich trough at which rent-seekers of various breeds come to feed"). R. Ellickson, *Three Systems of Land Use Control*, 13 Harvard Journal of Law and Public Policy 67, 73 (1990).

159. See McBain, *supra* note 156; Argument of Louis D. Brandeis, on behalf of the Massachusetts Protective Liquor Dealers' Association, before the Joint Committee on the Liquor Law of the Massachusetts Legislature, February 27, 1891, reprinted in 1 *Hearings on the Nomination of Louis D. Brandeis Before a Subcommittee of the Senate Committee on the Judiciary*, 1057, 1065 (1916).

160. City of Eastlake v. Forest City Ent., 426 U.S. 668, 672 (1976) (discussing problems relating to voting rights in local governments). See J. Goetz, *Direct Democracy in Land Use Planning*, 19 Pacific Law Journal 793 (1987).

161. Fischel, *supra* note 61, at 331; see J. Jacobs, *Economy of Cities* (1969).

162. Fischel, *Do Growth Controls Matter?, supra* note 146, at 55.

163. *Id.*

164. Fischel, *supra* note 61, at 235.

165. See Nelson, in Geisler and Popper *supra* note 61; and in Haar, *supra* note 61, at 311.

166. Nelson, in Haar, *supra* note 61, at 314.

167. *Id.* at 312.

168. *Id.* at 317.

169. Babcock and Larsen, *supra* note 63.

170. It is suggested that the proposers of a new district demonstrate: (1) why their area is unique; (2) why the standard zoning provisions would not meet their needs even if amended; (3) the extent of support and opposition; (4) the impacts on various citywide services and needs, such as housing, transportation, and services; and (5) why a more traditional historic district is not appropriate. *Id.*

171. R. Hawkins, *Neighborhood Policy: An Alternative to the Dominant Conception of Neighborhoods*, in *Neighborhood Policy and Planning* (P. Clay ed. 1983), at 193; see also R. Hawkins, *Self-Government by District* (1976), 116-17.

172. See M. Silver, *You Too Can Organize a Government*, 9 The Organizer no. L, at 25-29, 32-33.

173. A. Dunham, in *Law and Land: Anglo-American Planning Practice* (1964).

174. Nelson, in ACIR-RCA, *supra* note 30, at 50, both states and refutes this proposition. For other expressions of concern about the economically divisive effect of neighborhood groupings, see Isaac, *supra* note 68.

175. C. Mills, *The Power Elite* (1957), at 320.

176. *Id.*

177. P. Mann, *The Socially Balanced Neighborhood Unit*, 29 Town Planning Review 91 (1958).

178. P. Wolf, *Rethinking the Urban Street: Its Economic Context*, in *On Streets* (S. Anderson ed. 1978), at 377.

179. R. Gutman, *The Street Generation*, in *On Streets* (S. Anderson ed. 1978), at 249.

180. R. Putnam, *Making Democracy Work: Civic Culture in Italy* (1993), at 174; see also E. Banfield, *The Moral Basis of a Backward Society* (1958).

181. Mumford, *supra* note 19, at 260.

182. R. Dewey, *The Neighborhood, Urban Ecology and City Planners*, 15 American Sociological Review 502 (1950). The limited experiments with tenant management of social housing are described in D. Monti, *The Organization, Strengths and Weaknesses of Resident-Managed Public Housing Sites in the U.S.*, 11 Journal of Urban Affairs 1 (1989).

183. P. Smith, *As a City Upon a Hill, The Town in American History* (1968), at 199.

5

China—Tradition and Totalitarianism

The Chinese village, traditionally a highly organized social unit, possessed institutions that were co-opted by the new communist state, but that, by reason of the insularity and isolation of villages, retained some independence. The introduction of a market system and the commodification of land places these institutions under great pressure.

The Chinese urban dweller is subject to an elaborate system of social control through associations at the block and ward level, whose members are appointed and controlled from above. The system intensely mobilizes the efforts of women past childbearing age, and even more than the rural village dweller, the Chinese urban resident is subject to central control. While the government has not lost its commitment to neighborhood institutions, heightened internal migration and a market system separating residence from workplace will almost surely weaken them.

China provides the extreme case of the dangers inherent in small-scale governments whose officers are appointed from above and which are authorized to impose sanctions on individuals.

HISTORICAL BACKGROUND

The traditional organization of Chinese cities was not on a neighborhood basis, as in Japan, but in groups based on area of rural origin or occupation. However these primary associations frequently corresponded to patterns of residence within neighborhoods:

[A]ssociations organized residents to provide basic urban amenities, such as street sweeping and fire protection, and might close off gates at the end of the lane to protect residents at night. Typically a neighborhood shrine to the local earth god brought neighbors together for ritual occasions and reinforced local solidarity.[1]

THE 1949 REVOLUTION

With the chaotic conditions after the end of imperial rule, and explosive growth of cities, a breakdown of these structures ensued. When major cities fell to the Chinese Communists, a tightly knit organizational structure subordinated to Communist party control ensued. For the first four years from 1949 to 1953, ad hoc "people's tribunals" inflicted "revolutionary justice" on disfavored classes, sometimes in mass trials before hordes of onlookers. As in Russia, the sine qua non to this control was severe restriction on migration to cities, accompanied, as in the Russian case, by the murder or starvation of a large number of potential migrants. Families registered to live in cities are required to maintain registration books, duplicated at local police stations. Visitors must be reported to police stations as well. Booklets are called for inspection, and surprise nighttime inspections are conducted to enforce regulations. During the Cultural Revolution, large numbers of persons--in that case, 17 million of 100 million urbanites--were forced to move to the countryside.[2]

The effect of this was to create a condition of extreme residential stability. The average residence in the same urban house or apartment was as high as 18 years. Only 10% of persons had changed residence in the previous 5 years, as against 40% in the United States. Unlike the Soviet regulations, which applied only to Moscow and a few other cities, the restrictions on migration were pervasive.

These restrictions were accompanied by the organization of cities into districts of several hundred thousand people, wards of 2,000 to 10,000 families each, residents' committee units of 100 to 800 families, and small group units of 15 to 40 families in a single street or in a single building. The creation of these neighborhood groupings was regularized by an Act for the Organization of City Residents' Committees in 1954.[3] "At the level of the ward, there is a ward affairs office, a ward party committee or party branch, and a ward police station. These officials are paid and need not live in the neighborhood. The residents' committee members are appointed by ward leaders and are unpaid, except for the chairman, who receives a small stipend."[4] The designated leaders tend to be "females in their early fifties who received little education and typically never had a regular job."[5]

The police system is said to be inspired by the Japanese system.[6] In it, the ward police station is located next to the ward affairs office. However, in China the policing function is combined with a multitude of other economic subsistence, sanitation, welfare, and political functions . . . vital to everyday life. . . . The common joining of work and residence create the potential for high levels of solidarity and cooperation, crime control and social order, as well as a rapid remolding of the marriage customs, family patterns, fertility behavior and other social and intellectual habits of the citizenry. . . . However, the joining of so many police, economic, welfare and service functions into one massive bureaucracy also creates a potential for coercion, corruption, inefficiency, insensitivity to local needs, and personal vindictiveness by minor officials.[7]

In addition, the emphasis on workplace organization in China subtracts from neighborhood activity those who work elsewhere, leaving neighborhood groups to "housewives, children, unemployed youths, and retired workers."[8] The "work unit is responsible for most basic things of life, such as housing, medical care, child care and schooling, transportation, education and pension."[9]

To those features of neighborhood organization may be added some architectural factors, including little high-rise housing and "the use of doormen and gatekeepers in many buildings and organizations. . . . [n]eighborhoods often have a mixed character, with not only housing but shops, small factories . . . and other facilities."[10]

In addition to these passive factors, there are active measures of control, including neighborhood meetings to discuss government policy statements, household cleanliness inspections, and neighborhood sessions at which deviants are criticized. The appointed residents' committees engage in reporting to the police, recruit further informers, and report unknown visitors.[11] In total, "[though] the institution of criticism and self-criticism has its precedents in Soviet prescriptions . . . the thoroughness and depth of the Chinese Communist effort to integrate the individual into the collective by using the small group as an instrument of rectification and manipulation go well beyond Soviet practice."[12]

Because the neighborhood committees are appointed and dispose of few resources, it is said that they elicit a minimum degree of cooperation, rather than the active involvement that is desired.[13]

The scheme of control was significantly disrupted by the Cultural Revolution in which large numbers of youths involuntarily transferred to the countryside returned to the cities and hid out with their families, with the increasing complicity of neighborhood members, while remaining unemployed. In addition, neighborhood mediation and security committees ceased to function, though they were extensively revived by 1980.[14]

Neighborhoods were also frequently used to impose punishment that took the form of required writing of reports by offenders on their activities and assignment to tasks such as sweeping of lanes.[15] An elaborate hierarchy of penalties included criticism before groups of increasing size, required publicized self-criticism, and gradations of group abuse, verbal and physical. The more

intense sanctions were imposed by ordinary courts but carried out by neighborhood committees. In addition, persons might be required to periodically report
to the police and to seek police permission before traveling.[16] As the number
of persons experiencing these punishments increased, an ever-larger portion of
the population perceived themselves as victims rather than masters of the system.
One survey indicated that only a fourth of residents had a favorable view of
neighborhood leaders, most of whom "remained in office until they moved away,
died, or simply got too sick or decrepit to continue."[17] It was found in the
1970s that 84% of urban residential leaders (as against 45% of rural leaders) had
served for more than seven years, police supervision being much more pervasive
in urban areas.[18] The neighborhood apparatus was so thoroughly dominated by
the state "that neighborhood structures seemed to generate little enthusiasm,
interest or loyalty among the people."[19]

POST-REVOLUTIONARY REFORMS

Since 1976, the system has been reformed to the extent that there are
theoretically to be elections for membership on the residents' committee: "The
implementation of unit-level elections could be extremely disruptive whereas
county-level elections could occur almost unnoticed,"[20] though most officers
continue to be appointed.[21] Somewhat more free elections, from officially
approved lists, are held to elect large district congresses unable to impose "much
public supervision of the day-to-day work of formally appointed neighborhood
officers."[22] The effect of these controls has been to reduce, rather than enhance,
voluntary cooperation in urban areas. "Neighborhoods under tight control have
fewer ties among neighbors. . . . [T]here is the danger of conflict and political
attack from those who know too much about one."[23] By contrast, villages were
insulated from severe controls by "the small population of each unit, the kinship
basis of these units, their leadership by locals rather than outsiders, and their
considerable distance from police stations and other modes of internal control."[24] This led one commentator to stress the relative autonomy of the
villages under Mao's system and to observe that the "roles and behaviors of local
cadres, working at the lively intersection of state structure and village society,
may merit special attention."[25]

The result of the political controls is that "pride or attachment in intermediate
levels of urban organization are . . . weak."[26]

The picture of the system painted by Western commentators corresponds
rather closely to that once sought to be conveyed by the government itself. In
1980, an official description of the system depicted a representative committee
comprising ten neighborhood groups representing a total of 620 households and
2,100 residents. The chairman was said to be a woman of 70 with 30 years'
experience. The security committee chairman, a woman of 55, is said to be a

former head of the mediation committee and is "another old-timer in neighborhood work. . . . The other three assistant heads . . . are all middle-aged women."[27] Their functions are said to include instructions on killing mosquitoes and the use of rat poison. "[I]t's our duty to visit homes to see if the stores and flues are properly installed to avoid carbon monoxide poisoning"[28] and to see that preschool children are inoculated. The security committee "come[es] under the leadership of the local government agency at the lowest level and [is] also guided by the public security organs and people's courts."[29] Its members "are all local residents who know . . . who in the neighborhood have . . . disturbed the peace. Residents who find something amiss may report to the committee."[30] The official publication claims that in 1980 "members are elected directly by the local residents," but the election procedure is not described. "[I]n case of need a reasonable government subsidy may be granted."[31]

The counterpart to close relations between police and community is a network of informers.[32] The security defense committees thus operate to bring surveillance "down to the level of the individual household, a task which the single patrolman who is usually assigned to the area of a residents' committee would find it impossible to carry out."[33]

A sympathetic Marxist writer describes the system as having drastically curtailed its mediation function by rules adopted in 1957.

Mediation was explicitly limited to minor civil and criminal cases and any individual could bypass mediation and take his case directly to the court. . . . New legislation brought the committees under the control of an expanding semi-bureaucracy, the street office. . . . Residential small groups were henceforth the setting for gossip but little political action."[34]

While more power was granted mediation committees during the so-called Great Leap Forward in 1958 and the 1954 regulations were reissued in 1980[35], the change in leadership in 1962 insured that "popular participation in the residential committees and street offices dropped off."[36] With the advent of the Cultural Revolution, described by a sympathetic commentator as a "decade of reform,"[37] it was claimed that neighborhood elections involved "real political contest among a number of candidates."[38]

With the demise of Mao, the neighborhood organizations are said to have "declined in terms of influence and mass participation."[39] This shift may be ascribable to a view that the need for popular mobilization is past: "[S]hift in the citizen's role--from passive to active--is critical in a country starting on the road to modernization."[40] Under the new leadership, "state bureaucracies have been invested with sole regulatory power over administration and peace-keeping, while citizens' organizations are disbanded or reduced to auxiliary roles."[41]

In 1982, the political and economic functions of the rural communes were separated and a system of contracts with individual farmers inaugurated.[42] In

In 1982, the political and economic functions of the rural communes were separated and a system of contracts with individual farmers inaugurated.[42] In place of an economy based on an ideal of rural self-sufficiency, market institutions were instituted, lending to the suggestion that:

[i]n some respects, the socio-political changes accompanying the "liberal market" reforms of the 1980's may impair the ability of peasant communities to oppose inimical state actions and policies."[43]

THE ADVENT OF THE MARKET

While new local government units, shorn of economic functions, were given constitutional status in 1982, cities were merged with surrounding rural counties, thus ending, or at least relaxing, "the control of rural population mobility through the household registration system."[44] The reliance on the market, extending even to the commodification of land[45], and the creation of public labor markets for household services[46] "[have] shaken both the organizational skeleton of the honeycomb polity and the morality of localism that both legitimized and stiffened it."[47] There still remain "secret police, a comprehensive network of neighborhood and village organizations and a system of files to keep watch on all citizens," but the mutuality of interest that lent public support to the social structure in rural areas is in process of being destroyed.[48] This has not prevented, however, a renewed celebration of the neighborhood committee system in April 1990 and the enactment of an Organic Law of Urban Neighborhood Committees on 1 January, 1990. There are said to be 100,000 such committees, each including 100 to 700 households, carrying out functions such as study halls, probation supervision, organization of aged clubs, and operation of small stores, dining halls, garment workshops, bicycle parking lots, telephone booths, and house cleaning services.[49]

Nonetheless, whatever the dilution of the preexisting system that has taken place, there is much to be diluted. The devastating effect of informal sanctions is added to by the effective absence from Chinese criminal law of the principle of *nulla peona sine lege* that had begun to inform the Soviet system in the post-Stalin years.[50] Nor need the sanctions be in any way related to the offense:

the individual is not criticized for his specific refusal to volunteer. Rather the attack is a diffuse assault on his character and any kind of selfish undesirable behavior, including personal family and work history may be included as part of the denunciation. Because the attack is general rather than specifically related to a single act, the result can be far more devastating personally. . . . [W]elfare benefits for sickness, accidents and old age . . . are not guaranteed by the regime. . . . Special rations, sick pay, pharmaceutical needs, child care and so forth may all be determined by what the local census policeman has written in his little black book.[51]

NOTES

1. M. Whyte et al., *Urban Life in Contemporary China* (1984), at 12. See R. Lieberthal, *Revolution & Tradition in Tientsin* (1980); E. Vogel, *Canton Under Communism* (1969). For similar observations with respect to the overseas Chinese in Singapore, see C. Lim-Keah, *Social Change and the Chinese* (1985); T. Tan, *Political Modernization and the Traditional Chinese Voluntary Associations*, 13 Southeast Asian Journal of Social Sciences 67 (1985); *Voluntary Associations as a Model of Social Change*, 14 *Id.* 68 (1986). Also see J. Cohen, *The Criminal Process in China*, in *Soviet and Chinese Communism* (D. Treadgold ed. 1967), at 107, 110.

2. Whyte, *supra* note 1, at 20.

3. Cohen, in Treadgold, *supra* note 1, at 120.

4. *Id.* at 23. See also Salaff, *infra* note 8, at 292.

5. Salaff, *infra* note 8, at 283.

6. Cohen, *supra* note 1, at 23, citing D. Buck, *Urban Change in China* (1978).

7. *Id.* at 26.

8. J. Salaff, *Urban Residential Community in the Wake of the Cultural Revolution*, in *The City in Communist China* (J. Lewis ed. 1971), at 289.

9. R. Danquing et al., *Social Networks of Residents in Tianjan with a Comparison to Social Networks in America*, 11 Social Sciences in China 68 (1990).

10. Whyte et al., *supra* note 1, at 239.

11. *Id.* at 244.

12. M. Fainsod, *Transformations in the Soviet Communist Party*, in *Soviet & Chinese Communism* (D. Treadgold ed. 1967), at 70-71.

13. *Id.* at 245, citing Salaff, *supra* note 8.

14. *Id.* at 259; see also L. White, *Shanghai's Polity in Cultural Revolution*, in Lewis, *supra*, at 332-40.

15. Salaff, *supra* note 8, at 307.

16. Cohen, *supra* note 1, at 121-23, 128-29.

17. *Id.* at 281. See also Salaff, *supra* note 8, at 314.

18. Cohen, *Id.* at 286.

19. *Id.* at 290.

20. B. McCormick, *Political Reform in Post-Mao China* (1990), at 156.

21. Cohen, *supra* note 1, at 296. See McCormick, *supra* note 20, at 133-35.

22. Cohen, *supra* note 1, at 353.

23. *Id.* at 355.

24. *Id.* at 360. See also V. Shue, *The Reach of the State: Sketches of the Chinese Body Politic* (1988), also stressing the difference between rural and urban areas.

25. Shue, *supra* note 24, at 5.

26. *Id.*

27. Beijing News, 3 November, 1980, at 19-21. See also McCormick, *supra* note 20, at 117 n.81.

28. *Id.*

29. *Id.*

30. *Id.*

31. *Id.*

32. McCormick, *supra* note 20, at 119-20.

33. T. Cohen, *supra* note 1, at 121.

34. F. Brady, *Justice and Politics in People's China* (1982), at 127-28.

35. McCormick, *supra* note 20, at 115.

36. Brady, *supra* note 20, at 178.

37. *Id.* at 217.

38. *Id.* at 217.

39. *Id.* at 230.

40. E. Vogel, *Voluntarism and Social Controls*, in Treadgold, *supra* note 1, at 168.

41. Brady, *supra* note 34, at 246.

42. See Documents no. 1, 1984 (relating to rural communes), reprinted in China Quarterly (1985), at 184.

43. Shue, *supra* note 24, at 77. McCormick, *supra* note 20, at 4, likewise notes that "the Cultural Revolution's attack on institutional authority left in its wake pervasive networks of informal and personal authority, which are very difficult for central authorities to penetrate or control."

44. McCormick, *supra* note 20, at 115, 117.

45. See X. Liang, *Commercialization of Dwellings and Socialist Practice*, 7 Social Science in China 77 (1986)

46. 35 Beijing Review no. 5, at 43, 3 February, 1992. See also McCormick, *supra* note 20, at 1.

47. Shue, *supra* note 24, at 148.

48. *Id.* at 3.

49. Cheng Gang, *The Neighborhood Committee: Residents' Own Organization*, 33 Beijing Review, 9 April, 1990, at 30-32.

50. See Cohen, *supra* note 1, at 140.

51. Vogel, *supra* note 40, at 184.

6

Russia—Sovietism, its Roots and its Remnants

In Russia, the political institutions of rural areas were those of a collectivized and centrally administered agriculture, and the collectivism preceded the 1917 revolution. From all indications, the breakdown of this system is proceeding slowly at best.

In urban areas, the soviets, very large centrally appointed bodies at all levels of society, have been definitively abolished in favor of more conventional government structures. The same seems to be true of the institution of comrades' courts. Institutions such as the militia and residents' cooperatives appear to have survived the change of regimes, and concern for the growth of crime suggests that their role will not be greatly reduced. The important question for the future relates to the degree of their subservience to central power.

Many of the institutions popularly identified with the Soviet system, such as internal passports and farm collectives, had their origins in the Tsarist period. Under Joseph Stalin, reliance was placed on terror as a means of social control, and many communal institutions were permitted to wither, until their revival under Nikita Khrushchev, perhaps the last Marxist true believer. The fate of institutions such as the militia and house committees in post-Soviet Russia remains as an open question.

THE ROOTS OF SOVIET COLLECTIVISM

Although we are accustomed to thinking of the present state of Russian society as an ideological construct dating from 1917, in fact collectivism in Russia has deeper roots, in Russian serfdom and in the village mir that succeeded it. The period of serfdom was unaccompanied by strong regional institutions:

The state itself owned and exercised direct control over nearly half the present population and had transferred control of the other half to local gentry . . . [over] territories so large, so lacking in sharp distinctions and often so thinly populated as to hinder the development of strong regional institutions and loyalties.[1]

Upon emancipation, a regime was adopted in which taxes were laid upon the village as a collective unit.

[T]he periodic repartition of the communally held land and collective planting and harvesting fostered the same sort of mutuality, just as serfdom had as its end to bind individual peasants to a given village and its land. Such factors presented a high level of mutuality in the political life of the village by disarranging any strong manifestations of individualism.[2]

The repartition was "an effort to maximize the potential for meeting rising tax obligations."[3] "The political effects of this measure were debilitating. By denying the peasant the opportunity to own his land, the government deprived him also of the best school of political education. For the average citizen everywhere, the management of property, especially real estate, represents the main and sometimes only exercise in practical politics."[4]

Prerevolutionary rural Russian society thus was a society of local collectives ruled from above by an autocracy. Individual land tenure emerged with Stolypin's reforms, only to be reversed by the murderous collectivization campaign of 1929-32. In both the Tsarist and Communist periods, a system of internal passports restricted migration.

Although the literature of Marxism is singularly bereft of any concrete description of what social institutions would look like in the ultimate stage of communism, the closest approach to such descriptions appear in the writings of Marx and Lenin describing the process of revolution rather than its result. In the case of Marx, the utopian text is his celebration of the Paris Commune in *The Civil War in France*: "The Commune was to be a working, not a parliamentary academy, executive and legislative at the same time."[5] Lenin's utopia is that of State and Revolution, also purportedly descriptive of the Paris Commune:

[t]he gradual abolition of all bureaucracy . . . to replace the specific "bossing" of state officials by the simple functions of "foreman and accountants," functions which are already fully within the ability of the average town dweller and can be performed for workmen's wages.[6]

"The ideals of party life and party organization spring from a common source, and essentially they stress the possibility that all individuals, regardless of cultural or personal differences, can be modeled into the same disciplined revolutionary."[7]

This vision was to be carried out at the enterprise level. Nothing was said about territorial organization. By April 1918, having assumed power, Lenin was asking instead "that the people unquestioningly obey the single will of the leaders of labor."[8]

Although in some early writings, Lenin had drawn parallels between the commune and the soviets or committees of industrial workers elected at the time of the 1905 revolution,[9] this does not appear in his State and Revolution (written in July-August 1917) but made a brief reappearance after the Bolsheviks gained control of the soviets in September 1917, only thereafter to be submerged, most notably in the repudiation of democratic forms of government in *The Proletarian Revolution and the Renegade Kautsky*, written in October 1918.[10]

POST-REVOLUTIONARY SOVIETS

The Constitution of 10 July, 1918 thus retained soviets as a shadow representation of an ideal, not as organs with real power, a base of electoral units that were work units with territorial constituencies only for those not employed. They were to be elected upon a territorial rather than industrial base, and were in turn to indirectly elect higher instrumentalities up to the All-Russian Congress of Soviets. By the summer of 1918, parallel party organizations at each level had been erected, and by the Eighth Party Congress in 1919, a resolution was adopted proclaiming: "The party particularly strives to carry out its Programme and establish its complete control in the contemporary state organizations that are soviets."[11] By 1922, all parties, save the Communists, had been expelled from the soviets.

In general, town and village soviets were large bodies, with one deputy for every 1,000 inhabitants under the 1918 constitution, and one for every 100 citizens at the village level. Under the 1918 constitution, the town soviets were to meet once a week, the villages twice. In practice, as time went on, the soviets had largely dispensed with the holding of meetings, even for ceremonial purposes.[12] By 1936, the Moscow soviet had one delegate for every 1,500 voters, or a total of 2,116 persons; that of Kharkov had 1,900. It was claimed, apparently on the authority of a work by the notorious Lazar Kaganovich, that this body met every six to eight weeks for several days to adopt a resolution presented by its presidium and prepared by the Moscow Committee of the Communist party.[13] In addition, as of 1936 there were 23 subdistricts each with a district soviet with a total in Moscow of 5,935 members.[14] By 1985, 152 large cities were divided into district soviets, and there were a total of 52,041 local soviets with a total of 2,304,830 members.[15] In 1980, there were also said to be 2,727,000 volunteers serving on standing committees of local soviets.

It was said that by 1946, only 25 percent of the soviets held regular sessions. Between 1954 and 1957 the number of village soviets[16] was reduced from 73,737 to 50,265. In the Khrushchev era, the Communist party on 22 January 1957 adopted a resolution noting the desuetude of the soviets, which is regarded as a turning point in their history. By 1961, 95% of the Soviets held regular sessions, and the number of deputies had increased by about 400,000. Although in ensuing years there were efforts to curtail the soviets in favor of industrial and collective farm organizations, these efforts were not pressed to fruition. It was said that in 1980 that one-day sessions were required six times a year.[17]

In 1977, a new constitution laying greater stress on the work of the soviets was adopted, although it recognized democratic centralism and the dominant role of the party. It had been preceded by edicts of 8 April 1968 on village soviets and one of 12 March 1971 on urban ones, together with a law on the status of soviet deputies adopted on 10 September 1972.[18] While the reforms resulting from these changes were more theoretical than real, particularly in view of the strong position of local party organizations, they laid the groundwork for more meaningful reforms under Mikhail Gorbachev. In 1989, autonomous taxing powers for local soviets were proposed, together with the right to charge rents to industrial firms.[19] At least until this time

It [made] little sense even to speak of a city soviet, . . . rather the actual content of an urban complex consists of a collection of settlements each of which is attached to a large factory which is itself directly subordinate to some national ministry . . . Deputies of local soviets, realizing that to speak out against this state of affairs is to invite "subtle persecution" from the powers that be, have passively endured the economic exploitation of their respective territories and the ecological ruin that has usually accompanied it.[20]

Those regarding this apparatus as providing the basis of a civic culture pointed to a number of its features. First, the electing units adopted resolutions or mandates to their representatives containing requests for action, which must be acted on either affirmatively or negatively.[21] Second, representatives were expected to meet with[22] constituents at least once (since Article 20 of the 1979 Law on the Status of Deputies, twice) annually. Third, verbal complaints were possible at meetings of work units.[23] This led W. A. Robson in 1937 to applaud "the intimate relationship between the elector and his representative before, during and after election," while also noting "the permeation and control of the urban organization at its key points by the Communist Party,"[24] Robson alluding in his conclusion to "the spiritual fervor which is driving the Bolsheviks forward to great accomplishments" as well as "the fanatical intolerance which is holding them back."[25]

Sir E. D. Simon (later Lord Simon of Wythenshawe), a companion of Robson in 1937, took a more jaundiced view: "It is now abundantly clear that the so-called "instructions" are limited to such as are approved by the party. He acknowledged that "through the party membership, through the numerous elected soviets, through all kinds of committees in houses, factories, etc, it seems certain that a considerably larger proportion of the citizens of Moscow are getting training for democracy through experience of responsible public work than in London." However, after noting his observations of slave labor on the Moscow-Volga canal, he concluded:

The one-party system is a new form of dictatorship, like all dictatorships intolerant of criticism and opposition, but with the advantage over the old dictatorships of a large bank of devoted disciples, who serve the double purpose of keeping the leaders well informed as to public opinion and of guiding public opinion into the party line . . . helped by their full control of the ubiquitous and all-powerful police and of all the means of propaganda.[26]

With the Gorbachev era, the terror and monopoly of propaganda were removed, leading to the collapse of a system whose last defenders were some of the members of the soviets at all levels. Prior to the downfall of the system, it was established that the persons nominated were chosen by the party according to norms based on sex, age, occupation, and party background.[27]

The significant question for our inquiry relates to the downward reach of these large local legislatures and their relationship to the security apparatus. One benign form of downward reach is said to have been that to "review citizens' complaints in the sphere of housing, larger cities have created "deputies councils" on the territory of each housing operations office."[28]

THE MILITIA

Beginning in 1957, as part of Khrushchev's effort to broaden party organizations, *druzhiny*, or volunteer militia squads, were promoted with a formal resolution in 1959 "On the Participation of the Working People in the Preservation of Public Order" and were said to be "the most important voluntary organization in terms of membership today."[29]

These were organized by borough, under supervision of borough soviets and other organizations, and were usually enlisted at places of work to patrol against drunkenness and hooliganism by demanding identification from citizens, taking them to commanders, entering public places to maintain order, and reporting offenses to the press or on bulletin boards.[30] It is said that by 1965 there were 85,182 such units with 3,351,078 members. Their mass inspections "bring a crushing weight of conformity against those who, though not violating any law, are not acting in an approved manner."[31] In 1974, leadership of them was entrusted to the local soviets. An evening tour of duty was demanded once every six weeks or two months. Village assemblies were revived in 1961 after having been abolished in 1931.[32] The Gorbachev reforms proposed in 1984 moved to a territorial basis of election for soviets at all levels, except that one third of the seats were to be reserved for "public organizations."[33]

RESIDENTS' COMMITTEES

Finally, housing, street, and residential committees have long existed operating under the direction of the executive committee of the Soviet and "especially its Organizational Instructional Department."[34]

In 1960, such committees were said to have 29,000 to 50,000 members in Moscow and 30,000 in Leningrad. Committees enforced the internal passport regime.[35] These during the Stalin period were assuredly part of what has been described as "tight party and police supervision of urban employment and residence" as well as of "an unprecedented administrative apparatus of observation and terror",[36] vividly described in Anatoly Lvov's *The Courtyard*.[37] "An individual belongs to long-enduring vertically-structured groups that penetrate to a considerable extent into the private lives of their members and emphasize procedures for maintaining and restoring harmony . . . [but] the frequent exhortations to serve the collective operate in a less awesome way than in the years of Stalinism in favor of conformity in Russia."[38]

Beginning in 1959, strenuous efforts were made to revive residential organizations, with the chilling objective to "create in every home, in every apartment, such conditions that not a single amoral act by any one will go unnoticed."[39] While committee members were elected, a system of parallel party cells was created, and the election of members was subject to confirmation by the local Soviet.[40]

The committees, however, had as their main objective maintenance and repairs, political education, and the organization of leisure, not police-related functions.

COMRADES' COURTS

In 1959, a system of comrade's courts, previously used only for labor discipline, was given new emphasis. This system had come into existence in 1917 to harshly discipline recalcitrant workers, had been eliminated in October 1922 during the NEP (New Economic Plan) period, and had then been revived between 1928 and the purges with the different purpose of relieving the courts of minor cases. The RFSSR (Russian Federal Soviet Socialist Republic) statute extending the system to apartment houses was adopted on 30 June, 1933.[41] At the time of the purges, Andrei Vishinsky is reported to have declared that "the old twaddle about mobilizing activists from the ranks of the public and the formation of groups of volunteer helpers should be completely done away with; something else is needed now."[42]

However, the 1933 statute was never repealed, and a decree reorganizing the courts came into effect in the Russian Republic in 1961. The "courts" were set up on both occupational and territorial bases, the territorial basis including "an apartment building, or a complex of them, or a collective farm, or some other residential unit."[43] A 1965 study indicated that these bodies had more than half a million members.[44] It has been stated that "[r]enewed Soviet interest in the progressive transfer to 'social organizations' of the responsibility for imposing sanctions for violations of law and morality, which was prominently featured at the Twenty-first Party Congress in January 1959, may well have been spurred by Chinese experimentation with such forms."[45]

In theory, the state did not require comrades' courts, which might be set up by any residential unit with more than 50 persons with approval of the executive committee of the local soviet. Members were elected by the collective for one year; their jurisdiction extended to public conduct, minor damage to public property, violations of dwelling regulations, and various minor crimes. In October 1963, they were given additional jurisdiction over cases of petty theft, hooliganism, and speculation and first-time thefts of consumer goods from citizens belonging to the same collective as an offender. The 1961 and 1963 Russian Republic decrees, however, subjected the "Comrades Courts" to a considerable degree of legal regulation not present in the Chinese system.[46]

The "court" could require sanctions including restitution up to 50 rubles, public apology, public censure with or without publication in the press, fines up to 10 rubles, suggesting transfer or demotion to an employer, or eviction where the offense was premises related. It could also refer matters to ordinary criminal authorities. The executive committee of the local soviet might review the disposition; execution of monetary sanctions was through the ordinary courts.[47]

There was soviet criticism of the courts on two counts: that they were on occasion used to settle private scores or that public authorities used them to lighten ordinary dockets. A Western critic has noted that the lay courts were a soviet response to "problems of industrialization, urbanization and post-adolescent rebellion that are encountered in not very dissimilar forms in Britain, the United States, and many other countries."

Nonetheless, it is clear that the popularization of justice tends to bring an even larger portion of life under the eye of a watchful regime. The freedom of ordinary civil life, where work, play, family, public service, social life can be kept in separate though not completely sealed compartments, is infringed in the total institution for the subject's own good as the institution views it. To a lawyer, the closest parallel in a looser society is the process by which a convicted defendant is sentenced.[48]

The same commentator notes another, perhaps less controversial soviet innovation: the release of offenders on probation to a collective unit, usually a work unit or collective farm.[49]

The revival of the militia and of comrades' courts has been interpreted as part of

a more mature stage of development in which the party put less reliance on coercive mobilization and more on incentives, welfare benefits and social pressure to achieve its objectives. With the abandonment of large-scale terror there is greater reliance on indoctrination, persuasion and such forms of social pressure as the comrade's courts, the druzhiny, or people's guards and the anti-parasite tribunals to discourage deviant social behavior.[50]

The use of these instrumentalities in the early experimental phase of the system and later in its liberalizing phase was a substitute for, not an adjunct to, terror. The essence of social control, and the basis of terror, is an effort to divide individuals from one another and disintegrate sources of potential opposition. The creation of communal institutions, however well controlled, is in some measure inconsistent with this logic.

HOUSING PROJECTS

In addition to security committees, there are other residence committees that "carry on general mobilizations for clean-ups, tree plantings, organization of meetings at elections time, and the like."[51] Other groups "carry out routine maintenance and repairs in housing projects, relieving the over-burdened municipal housing repair administrations."[52] In addition, house committees in housing projects operate "libraries, day care centers, and playgrounds . . . staffed almost completely by pensioners," and parents' committees attempt to extend the school system's effectiveness and unify it with the home and the recreational environment."[53]

The social integration of communities has also been attempted through architectural means. In the Khrushchev era the Stalinist practice of building monumental apartment buildings along wide boulevards was abandoned in favor of five-story walk-up buildings arranged in microdistricts of about 5,000 to 20,000 residents, including a school, kindergartens and nurseries, shopping areas, and parkland.[54]

RECENT DEVELOPMENTS

The advent of the Yeltsin era has seen significant change in some of these institutions and continuity in others. A draft constitution proposed by Yeltsin on

16 June, 1993 appears to effectively abolish comrade's courts by providing (Article 113): "Justice is administered only by the courts."[55] By a decree On the Right of Russian Federation Citizens to Freedom of Movement, dated 6 October, 1993, the residence permit system was abolished, though registration at police stations (which may not be refused) is still required. This step was taken over the objection of the Moscow authorities, who were assured, however, that they could continue to give existing residents preferences in allocation of housing.[56] The significance of the change is thus in doubt, in a society in which public authorities control a near-monopoly of housing. As was observed nearly 30 years ago: "Control over labor force size by this [internal passport] means is far less certain than control by regulation of housing space assignments in a given locality. Employers in need of labor may ignore the failure of a job applicant to receive his [residency permit] and may even help him make housing arrangements."[57]

On the other hand, a resolution of Prime Minister Chernomyrdin dated 20 September, 1993 revives the use of volunteer police aides citing a Council of Ministers resolution of 19 June 1974. The resolution also indicates that a Law on Public Participation in the Maintenance of Law and Order will shortly be adopted.[58]

One uncharacteristic development of the Soviet period was the revival of housing cooperatives whose precursors, leasing cooperatives, had been effectively abolished by a 17 October, 1937 decree prohibiting loans to them because of the "new political policy which emphasized administrative and political centralization at the expense of individual and institutional autonomy, to which the leasing co operative had given rise and encouraged."[59] In July 1957 a decree "on developing housing construction in the USSR" permitted loans to cooperatives of citizens creating multiapartment houses, as a means of soaking up public savings. A decree in this sense was issued on 20 March, 1958. It stipulated that only state construction organizations could erect buildings for cooperatives. In 1962, regulations were liberalized, while at the same time individual house construction was virtually prohibited. By 1965, about 6 to 7% of housing construction in the USSR was of the cooperative type. In the Russian Republic, cooperatives could be established by 24 to 60 citizens. When established, 40% of construction costs had to be paid before construction could begin. On completion, the carpenter receives an apartment and has a right to participate in management and to transfer his apartment to any adult relative who lives with him. The cooperative movement was essentially a movement of the well-to-do.[60]

Finally, although nothing in contemporary Russia is necessarily final, the city, borough, and district soviets themselves--bastions of the old order notwithstanding their large number of members--were abolished by a decree of President Yeltsin On the Reform of Local Self-Government in the Russian Federation, dated 26 October, 1993. Their functions were transferred to local governmental bodies, which held elections during the period from December 1993 to June 1994.[61]

NOTES

1. C. Black et al., *The Modernization of Japan and Russia: A Comparative Study* (1975), at 43.

2. *Id.* at 3.

3. *Id.* For a description of the village mir, see R. Ellickson, *Property in Land*, 102 Yale Law Journal 1315, 1393-94 (1993).

4. R. Pipes, *Communism and Russian History*, in *Soviet and Chinese Communism: Similarities and Differences* (1967), at 3, 13-14.

5. The Lennist texts on this point are usefully collected in T. Cooke and P. Morgan, *Participatory Democracy* (1971), at 149-83.

6. *Id.*

7. C. Pye, in Treadgold, *supra* note 4, at 39.

8. Cooke, *supra* note 5.

9. J. Hahn, *Soviet Grassroots: Citizen Participation in Local Soviet Government* (1988), at 60, citing V. Lenin, *Lessons of the Commune*, 23 March 1908, in Lenin, 13 *Collected Works*, vol. 13, p. 478.

10. *Id.* at 61, citing Lenin, 28 *Collected Works*, at 231-42.

11. *Id.* at 64-65. The Program of the Eighth Party Congress of July 1919 declared: "In the Soviet state not a territorial district but a productive unit (factory mill) forms the electoral unit of the state." From L. Churchward, *Public Participation in the USSR*, in Soviet Politics and Government (E. Jacobs ed. 1983), at 35.

12. M. Urban, *More Power to the Soviets: The Democratic Revolution in the USSR* (1990), at 3.

13. W. Robson, *A General View of the City Government of Moscow*, in *Moscow in the Making* (E. Simon ed. 1937), at 2.

14. *Id.* at 30.

15. J. Hahn, *supra* note 9, at 86.

16. *Id.* at 71. See Jacobs, *supra* note 11. Introduction at 15, R. Hill, *The Development of Soviet Local Government since Stalin's Death,* in Jacobs *supra* note 11, at 23.

17. Hill, *supra* note 16, at 72. See Jacobs, *supra* note 11, at 10, 24.

18. Hahn, *supra,* at 14. See Hill, *supra* note 16, at 30.

19. Urban, *supra* note 12, at 151.

20. *Id.,* at 147.

21. Robson, *supra* note 13, at 8. Provision for this was added as Article 102 to the 1977 constitution and an edict of 1 September, 1980. Churchward, *supra* note 11, at 44. See Hahn, *supra* note 9, at 135-49.

22. Robson, *supra* note 13, at 9; Hahn, *supra* note 9, 149-57.

23. Robson, *supra* note 13, at 54; Hahn, *supra* note 9, 157-68.

24. Robson, *supra* note 13, at 64. On the continued inconsequence of the legislative role of soviets, see T. Friedgut, *A Local Soviet at Work,* in Jacobs, *supra* note 11, at 157.

25. Robson, *supra* note 13, at 67.

26. E. Simon, *The Mossoviet: Is It Democratic?* in Simon *supra* note 13, at 225.

27. Jacobs, *supra* note 11, at 80.

28. *Id* at 17.

29. L. Churchward, *supra* note 11, at 38.

30. L. Lipson, *Law: The Function of Extra-Judicial Mechanisms in the USSR,* in T. Cooke and Morgan, *supra* note 6, at 453-54.

31. Friedgut, *infra* note 34, at 244, 257-62.

32. L. Churchward, *supra* note 11, at 38. These were committees elected for two and a half years, which met "as an extension of the executive committee of the village Soviet." *Id.* at 42. In theory, the assemblies could be convened by 20% of the inhabitants at their own initiative. Hahn, *supra* note 9, at 173-74.

33. Urban, *supra* note 12, ch. 3 and 4.

34. Hahn, *supra* note 9, at 169; T. Friedgut, *Political Participation in the USSR* (1979), at 235-88; W. Odom, *The Soviet Volunteers* (1973).

35. Friedgut, *supra* note 34, at 262-67.

36. C. Black et al., *supra* note 1, at 215.

37. A. Lvov, *The Courtyard* (1989).

38. Black et al., *supra* note 31, at 318, 337.

39. A. Unger, *Soviet Mass Political Work in Residential Areas*, 22 Soviet Studies 556 (1970).

40. R. Wesson, *Volunteers and Soviets*, 15 Soviet Studies 231, 233 (1963). For a description of the *domkoms*, or residential committees, see A. DiMaio, *Soviet Urban Housing* (1974), at 165, 72, concluding that "the ispolkom, trade union committees and especially the leaders of the housing organizations pay the domkom little mind."

41. R. Boiter, *Comradely Justice: How Durable Is It?* 14 Problems of Communism 82 (1965).

42. *Id.*

43. *Id.*

44. Friedgut, *supra* note 34, at 247.

45. J. Cohen, *The Criminal Process in China*, in *Soviet and Chinese Communism* (D. Treadgold ed. 1967), at 140.

46. H. Berman and Spindler, *Soviet Comrades' Courts*, 38 Washington Law Review 842 (1963).

47. Lipson, *supra* note 30, at 144-67.

48. *Id.* See also Friedgut, *supra* note 34, at 249-57.

49. Lipson, *supra* note 30.

50. M. Fainsod, *Transformation in the Soviet Communist Party*, in Treadgold, *supra* note 4, at 42, 65, 68.

51. R. Osborn, *Soviet Social Policies* (1970), at 243-58.

52. Friedgut, *supra* note 34, at 274.

53. *Id.* at 276.

54. *Id.* at 277.

55. 45 Current Digest of the Post Soviet-Press, no. 20, (16 June, 1993), at 18.

56. 45 Current Digest of the Post-Soviet Press, no. 36 (6 October, 1993), at 22.

57. Osborn, *supra* note 51, at 205.

58. 45 Current Digest of the Post-Soviet Press, no. 38 (20 October, 1993), at 24, citing Izvestia, 24 September, 1993, at 2.

59. Andrusz, *Housing and Urban Development in the USSR* (1984), at 40.

60. DiMaio, *supra* note 40, at 105-92. On the earlier history, see Andrusz, *supra* note 59, at 37-42.

61. 45 Current Digest of the Post-Soviet Press, no. 43, (24 November, 1993), at 17, citing Izvestia, 28 October, 1993, at 1.

7

Japan—Traditional Institutions Revitalized

The village institutions of medieval Japan have survived into modern times and continue to perform many social functions. Even compulsory labor on public roads has survived for longer than in any Western industrialized state.

The institutions of urban Japan are less typical and more instructive. These include centrally run law enforcement institutions with drastically decentralized administration and pervasive representation in every neighborhood. Alongside these is an elected structure of neighborhood social service organization that has been separated from the state but figures heavily in its strategy for the care of young and old and goes far to explain the low levels of general taxation in Japan.

Among democratic nations, Japan is the country in which the villagelike institutions of traditional society have best survived in modernized form. Their adaptation, however, owes a surprising amount to Western influence.

TRADITIONAL INSTITUTIONS

The foundation of a centralized Japanese state took place in the late 1860s and was closely followed by compulsory conscription. A House Registration decree to implement conscription was adopted in 1871, the nation being divided into administrative districts, each encompassing a number of the natural villages of the earlier period. In the earlier period, the assessable yield of a village would be determined by a land survey, and the village would be collectively taxed.[1] The offices of the traditional village headmen were formally abolished in 1872. In 1873 a Department of Home Affairs, important until after the war, was established. The traditional village system with grouping of five to ten families, further organized into block and village groupings, is said to date from the seventh century and to have been an import from China.[2]

In 1878, four decrees were promulgated that abolished the approximately 8,000 districts then existing and, in some measure, restored a village system.[3] Although the village heads were in theory to be elected, this apparent liberalization was qualified by requiring their approval by an appointed governor. In 1884, elections were further limited by requiring the village assemblies to nominate three candidates, of whom the governor appointed one.

In 1888, a codification of rules for local government, heavily influenced by the Prussian example, was placed in effect.[4]   Its Japanese draftsmen were heavily influenced by the writings of Rudolf Gniest, Albert Mosse (who came to Japan as an adviser in 1886), and Vom Stein.[5] The General Principles for the Reform of the Local Government System was the work of Mosse.[6] The result was a reform in which towns and villages elected their mayors, larger cities had their mayors appointed from lists of three, and the three largest cities were to be administered by appointive officials. At the same time, a series of compulsory amalgamations of villages was carried out, reducing their number from more than 70,000 to 15,820. "These new administrative villages were so preoccupied with . . . delegated functions that they were not really able to take over the self-governing powers of the older villages."[7]

However, the old village did not disappear altogether.[8] It remained the center of loyalty and identification for its inhabitants, retained its social importance as a unit of cooperative living, and stayed as independent within the new administrative units as was feasible. "Even today . . . village boundaries, although they have lost all administrative significance whatever, are still something that villagers are usually aware of . . . [T]his is a particularly Japanese characteristic, not to be found in other Asian countries, such as China and India."[9]

By Home Ministry Ordinance no. 17 of September 1940, the preexisting villages were revived[10] with the aim, expressed several years earlier by the War and Navy ministers, of freeing the country from "individualistic institutions and liberalistic policies,"[11] a part of a "Villages Fit for an Empire Movement."[12] While preexisting village groupings were universal, their urban equivalents were prevalent in only about a third of urban areas, primarily those of small shopkeepers. Under the government's design, the villages and block associations each had beneath them entities called *tonariqumi* or *gominqumi* consisting of about five to ten households, 10 to 20 such entities making up a village or block association of 100 to 200 households.[13] By April 1941, a total of 199,700 block associations and 1,120,000 *tonariqumi* had been created, and were given formal recognition by a law of 27 February, 1942. "Households were responsible for their own welfare, and matters the family could not cope with were taken care of by local communitarian associations; there was very little consideration for building the institutions and installations of a social and public character that are necessary in large cities."[14]

These entities were rigidly controlled from above. The *tonariqumi* disseminated official instructions, distributed rations, and collected taxes. The leaders of block associations were appointed by the mayor from persons nominated by the group. This apparatus "provided a ready force of security information to the authorities."[15]

THE OCCUPATION

Upon the advent of the Occupation, the system was initially put to use by the Occupation authorities, some 512 instructions being transmitted through urban block associations between August 1945 and May 1946. The initial effort of the Occupation authorities was to render the neighborhood associations elective. By November of 1946, only about one ninth of the previous heads of Tokyo associations had been replaced. Since the Occupation authorities were pressing for a purge of the 220,000 association executives, the Yoshida government undertook to avoid this by describing the associations as "voluntary associations."[16] This effort was unsuccessful, the purge being extended to the local level by Imperial Ordinance no. 4 of 4 January, 1947, which also provided for election of association heads in April 1947.

In a further effort to avoid formal elections, Home Ministry Instruction of 22 January, 1947 transferred all administrative tasks to public entities by 1 April, 1947, staple food rations to be issued directly to the individual consumer rather than through block associations. At the same time, however, the Home Ministry indicated that abolition of the governmental functions of the associations "opened the road for reformation of free voluntary organizations of the citizens for the satisfaction of their needs." It was also made clear that the upward transfer of power to cities, towns, and wards still permitted "subordinate members of a staff of city, town or ward [to] be assigned to suitable districts,"[17] which generally corresponded with former association areas.

This intransigence led to a Cabinet order of 3 May, 1947 promulgated at the direction of the Occupation authorities. All officers of neighborhood associations who had served continuously from 1 September, 1945 to 1 September, 1946 were barred from similar municipal functions. Municipal officers were forbidden to issue orders to association heads, who in turn were forbidden to issue orders to members or withhold rations from them. Associations formed after 22 January, 1947 were required to be dissolved by 31 May, 1947.

It has been observed that "the five year interdiction had little effect on actual practice in rural Japan."[18] On 24 October, 1952, the ordinance outlawing the associations became void when Law 18 of April 1952 keeping Occupation ordinances in effect for 180 days expired. Article 68 of the Local Government Law thus was operative in providing that "for purposes of administrative convenience, subdivisions of towns and villages may be created and a division chief and one deputy may be appointed."[19] Even more explicit recognition was accorded the old entities to the extent that they owned real property by the recognition of so-called "property wards" by the Local Autonomy Law.[20] Since as of 1910, 41,000 of the 76,000 then existing villages owned property, this recognition would have been of some importance even if the preexisting entities had not survived for other purposes. In addition, Article 260 of the Local Autonomy Law continues to provide for notice of name changes of the associations.

Notwithstanding the limited legal recognition of Japanese neighborhood associations, they continue to be of great social importance. A survey in 1955 revealed that as of that late date a system of compelled labor on roads strikingly reminiscent of the former parish system in England survived in Japanese villages.

The most universal form [of service] was road-mending, usually carried out twice a year, in spring and autumn. 94 percent of hamlets covered in the 1955 survey had such a system and in nearly all of these (96 percent to be precise) each household was expected to send one person to join the work gang. This is still usually unpaid labor; only 11 percent of hamlets paid a work allowance and that usually a token amount. It is estimated that the average hamlet requires some six days a year of unpaid labor from each household.[21]

As in England a century earlier, however, "hamlet work has become a synonym for slack and inefficient work."[22]

In spite of the hostility of the Occupation authorities to the neighborhood associations, they were not without their defenders during the Occupation period, one of whom described them as "a force in democratic education,"[23] a second of whom observed that "we abolished the essentially democratic neighborhood associations because they had been misused during the war,"[24] and a third of whom saw them as "a Catholic way for Japan."[25] The critics of the associations took the view that "they had survived as a vicious exploitative national intelligence system and a tyrannical means of enforcing collective responsibility for and control over the activities of individual citizens."[26] A Japanese critic in 1952 referred to them as "overrun by men of dubious character, extorting fees and donations under compulsion without clarifying their disbursement, liable to be exploited at election time."[27]

It is in any event clear that the attempts to outlaw the associations were unsuccessful.

According to a survey by the Autonomy Board in 1956, organizations similar to the outlawed neighborhood associations in area and function were established within three months of the abolition in 94 percent of the rural areas and in 77.9 percent of the country as a whole . . . More than 90 percent of the associations performed such functions as collective expressions of congratulation or condolence, the prevention of crimes, the distribution of insecticide, and the carrying out of tasks delegated by Ward Officials.

Cooperation in the big spring house-cleaning campaign in road and ditch cleaning, in fire protection and in night-watch services were frequent functions. At least half of the associations organized shrine festivals, parties to pay respect to old people, or other recreational affairs."[28]

A study of associations in new suburban developments lists such functions as weekly open air markets, collective purchasing and bill paying, and organization of the employment of a neighborhood barber.[29]

POST-OCCUPATION CHANGES

Following the end of the Occupation, the chief of the Administrative Division of the Autonomy Board declared that there was "no positive intention at present to reconstruct the neighborhood associations as administrative units. . . . their revival would be neither encouraged nor forbidden."[30] In fact, their revival has been pervasive and locally encouraged.[31] Many of the urban groups, calling themselves crime prevention associations, receive aid from the police in the form of subsidies and office space.

The rise of a new blue-collar and white-collar class has somewhat diminished the significance of neighborhood organizations, "which continue to be dominated by the remaining family enterprises." For these groups, "there is a strong tendency to find reference groups in, and to conform to the society of, the workplace."[32]

A critic of the associations wrote in 1978: "Political life is still based on a system of local conservatism operated through rural-style neighborhood associations, a system where a local power elite is active in Diet members' supporters associations or local chapters of pressure groups, and remains dependent on a control system managed by central government bureaucrats."[33]

CRIME PREVENTION ASSOCIATIONS

There are said to be not less than 1,200 crime prevention associations, known as *Bohan Kyokai.* Approximately 1 house in 50 is designated as a "contact point" for law enforcement purposes: "a residence or business, designated by small green or yellow signs fixed near the door, where people solicit police help or obtain information",[34] there being some 560,000 such "contact points" in Japan. Typically, the size of the neighborhood associations is quite small. Some 87.9% of the associations in villages were composed of fewer than 150 families, as were 66.4% of those in midsized cities and 26.5% of those in the six largest cities.[35] Of the large-city associations, only 27.9% had more than 500 families, and the proportion of large associations in midsized cities was only 3.7%.[36]

These new officially stimulated groupings in some measure supplant the traditional urban and rural units, which also have been supplemented on the newer housing estates by estate self-governing associations, which were said to impose less "constraining bands of a community character."[37]

POLICE ORGANIZATIONS

The crime prevention associations are paralleled by similarly numerous traffic safety associations, also of a theoretically private but locally assisted nature. The associations dovetail closely with the system of police posts that characterizes the Japanese policing system. Notwithstanding efforts during the Occupation to decentralize control of law enforcement, the police were recentralized immediately following the end of the Occupation.[38] "No issue concerned the ex-bureaucrats more in the first half of the 1950's than the recentralization of the nation's police forces."[39] While police forces are organized at the prefecture level and national funds account for only about 10% of their expenditures, the chief of each prefecture and two of his deputies are national civil servants, the riot police and security police are national agencies, and the national government pays for senior salaries, training, communications, identification laboratories, and statistical work. One of the prime minister's three secretaries is a career police officer.[40]

Functionally, however, the Japanese police are decentralized to the neighborhood level in accordance with the recommendations of a Prussian police official in 1891[41] and are organized in 5,800 *Kobans*, or urban police stations, each measuring about one-fourth square mile, with an average population of 11,500 and 10,000 rural chuzaisko, or residential police stations, each serving an average of 19 square miles with 7,890 people.[42] "The Japanese, disdaining the economics of the patrol car, kept a vision of the social function of police posts.[43] "Twice a year uniformed policemen knock on the door of every residence in Japan and ask questions about the people living there," [44] a practice that has existed since 1874.[45] In addition, the police posts maintain close contact with neighborhood associations, although it is said that "arrests that began with a tip were only 4.5 percent of all arrests for theft in urban areas in 1975,"[46] notwithstanding that the police pay "checkpoint" families for tips. Many original practices were modeled after those of the nineteenth century French police.[47]

In other ways, however, the outreach of the Japanese police is wider than that resulting from the more bureaucratic approach of their Western counterparts. Crime prevention fliers are circulated through neighborhood associations. Semiannual traffic safety campaigns are conducted, and volunteer traffic assistants are chosen on the basis of recommendations from neighborhood association heads. In a fashion reminiscent of Fielding's "hue and cry" in eighteenth-century England, "the media broadcast descriptions of criminals most wanted by the police;" in addition, posters of wanted criminals are placed "in train stations, public bath houses, and elsewhere where people gather,"[48] juvenile officers patrol shopping malls and parks looking for young runaways, and police call on the shut-in elderly and on accident victims in hospitals. As is sometimes true in rural areas in America, the police on occasion adopt a program "of publishing in the morning newspapers the names, addresses and companies of people apprehended for driving while drunk the night before."[49] "If juvenile unit officers notice a youth smoking, they take his cigarettes and counsel him not to smoke, they find out where he obtained his cigarettes and inform his parents of his behavior."[50] These and other "age-old social constraints limit individuality and often hamper self-fulfillment, as does life in a village, though they are effective means of social control."[51]

There is also a striking degree of citizen involvement in the treatment of offenders. There are 56,000 volunteer probation officers organized into 764 local units, in addition to a network of volunteer counsellors for narcotics addicts. "There is no obligation on these counsellors to report an addict to law enforcement agencies."[52] One community in 1974 is said to have had only 12 professional probation officers to supplement 954 volunteers. [53]

An admirer of the Japanese system has observed:

Americans, by contrast, react [to crime] as private individuals, purchasing guns, raising dogs, and buying security devices. Apart from paying taxes, Americans cannot conceive contributing to public security other than through acts of individual self-defense. This is one reason why private gun ownership is so important in the United States. Americans, for all their reputation as joiners, have virtually no organizations that provide assistance to the police on a day-to-day basis."[54]

Another observer noted:

There is a space between legality and propriety. Japanese policemen are not afraid to trespass there, their characteristic action being to exhort and admonish. . . . [P]articularistic loyalties of individuals to families and small communities have been transferred to new groups in the years since 1868. . . . This suggests, referring to the United States, that informal sanctions are attenuated not because of industrialization but because of a traditional insistence on individualism.[55]

To a remarkable degree, Japan has used official policy to arrest the decline in importance of neighborhood that ordinarily accompanies modernization. Surveys in 1973 and 1978 showed that when asked what institutions they could rely upon to discuss and help each other over anything and everything, 32% of the respondents identified the neighborhood and 55% the workplace.[56]

While most commentators are cautious about the transferability of Japanese practices to the West, it has been noted that "[t]here is no cultural inhibition in the U.S. against expanding the duration of police training to a year [as in Japan] or setting up counselling offices. . . . The police could make a major contribution to transforming the public's view of the utility of firearms for private protection."[57]

Summing up virtues and defects, Clifford writes:

[A] study of the socialist countries would probably reveal a basic correspondence to Japan in terms of the crime prevention form of social subdivision into small neighborhood or employment groups with close police links . . . Certainly this tighter neighborhood control and this development of the employment and residential pattern as a reference for behavior can be overdone if individual freedom is the objective, but it is surely a system as amenable to organization from "below" in the Western tradition as it is appropriate to the Japanese organization of it from "above."[58]

Similarly, a comparative study of Japan and Russia ascribed their common emphasis on collective organization to "the cooperative preparation and upkeep of rice paddies" in Japan and the "periodic repartition of communally held land and collective planting and harvesting" in early Russia.[59] Their relative success in modernization was ascribed to the "tight party and police supervision of urban employment and residence" in Russia and the "noted system of neighborhood or ward associations" in Japan, which allowed newcomers "to identify and to be identified in cities."[60]

COMMUNITY CARE

In 1969, a subcommittee of the Japanese People's Welfare Council issued a report entitled "Komyuniti: Regaining a Sense of Humanity in the Places Where Life Is Lived," which even Fukutake, a liberal and a pessimist among Japanese sociologists, concedes

had some small reflection in the subsequent orientation of administrative policies. . .
. [A]s current discussions of the increasing importance of community care always assume, the poor and handicapped need communities. . . . The problems which the small marital home of today cannot deal with, the problems of the handicapped and of bedridden old people, need a community solution, the development of some kind of organized cooperative care."[61]

Cities now typically publish suggested bylaws, listings of available subsidies, and procedures for communication of information to associations. They also conduct annual meetings with neighborhood representatives.[62]

In addition, as a matter of national policy, embodied in a Law Governing Volunteer Workers in Welfare Services, community care for the aged is organized to the neighborhood association level. Professional social workers are not involved in this process, which involves engagement for three-year terms of volunteer workers, each of whom works with the elderly 100 days a year, participates in monthly district meetings, and receives a nominal stipend and invitations to community functions.[63]

A policy of active subsidization of old people's clubs increased the level of participation of persons over the age of 60 from 12.8% in 1962 to 47.2% in 1973.[64]

Japan has been aided in her adaptation to modernity by two attributes, one rooted in history and one replicable elsewhere. "First, there is the tendency for Japanese associations and organizations to be territorially based. . . . [S]econd is their strong connection with various levels of government and public administration."[65] In addition, the tradition of lifetime employment has had some of the same effects on mobility and migration as the explicit controls on migration imposed in China and Russia. "The limited scope for the Japanese to change their employment helps greatly in keeping society under survey."[66] Nonetheless, the society is not impervious to change, and one observer has concluded:

An attempt to strengthen authoritarian leadership in city ward associations is not likely to be easy, for the opposition had deeper causes than the mere ideological influence or top-level institutional changes of the Occupation years. It is the product of a complex of changes--the increasing division of labour, the attenuation of economic links among city neighbors, the tendency for stratification, to follow occupation lines as part of a nationwide and not merely a local system and the institutionalization of equality of opportunity in the educational system--changes which cannot be easily revised.[67]

PROMOTION OF EXTENDED FAMILIES

The fostering of the extended family is another means whereby residential mobility is minimized. While the percentage of elderly persons living with their children has begun to decline, it is still far higher than in the United States or Western Europe. Income tax credits are given to children supporting a parent in their home, and loans are "provided for care givers who build or remodel a house with an independent room for older parents, or add such a room to an existing home."[68] In addition the construction of three-story buildings was conditioned on the requirement that

there be separate access for the two families to the building as well as separate kitchens and bathrooms. . . . The higher degree of autonomy offered by these new houses directly relates to the traditional fears of the younger married couple, particularly the wife, of excessive subservience to aging parents or in-laws. . . . [I]n November, 1988, the Building Standards Law was amended to permit three-story timber frame construction within areas not designated for fireproof or semi-fire-resistant buildings."[69]

The Japanese have thus repeatedly demonstrated impressive powers of adaptation. The pressures on them--some of them external and of dubious wisdom--to rationalize their agriculture and system of small-shop distribution, may render their future society more mobile than it is at present, as may the economic pressures breaking down the system of lifetime employment. Even, or perhaps especially, in this situation, the tradition of territorial neighborhood association may be of value:

Many people develop informal ties with their neighbors which are of emotional and mutual value to them only because the formal institutions of the ward association and the tonari-guri give them a means of breaking the ice. The insecure new immigrant from the country . . . may find great comfort in the assurance of help from neighbors. . . . Though attenuated, some sense of "belonging" to the ward, annually stimulated by the gaiety of the two-day festival celebrations, may well enrich the lives of some people and help to contact the generally deplored psychological effects of the increasing atomization and depersonalization of city life.[70]

NOTES

1. T. Fukutake, *The Japanese Social Structure: Its Evolution in the Modern Century* (1982), at 34.

2. K. Steiner, *Local Government in Japan* (1965), at 24. See SCAP, infra note 27, at 285.

3. Steiner, *supra* note 2, at 30.

4. *Id.* at 34.

5. *Id.* at 36.

6. *Id.* at 39.

7. Fukutake, *supra* note 1, at 34.

8. *Id.* at 46.

9. *Id.* at 34.

10. *Id.* at 47.

11. *Id.* at 57.

12. *Id.* at 38.

13. *Id.* at 59; also at 38. See W. Clifford, *Crime Control in Japan* (1976), at 99.

14. Fukutake, *supra* note 8, at 104.

15. Clifford, *supra* note 13, at 99.

16. Steiner, *supra* note 2, at 73.

17. *Id.* at 74.

18. R. Beardsley et al., *Village Japan* (1959), at 351.

19. T. Fukutake, *Japanese Rural Society* (1967), at 118.

20. Steiner, *supra* note 2, at 201.

21. Fukutake, *supra* note 19, at 129. See T. Smith, *The Agrarian Origins of Modern Japan* (1959).

22. Fukutake, *supra* note 19, at 136.

23. R. Braibanti, *Neighborhood Associations in Japan and Their Democratic Potentialities,* 7 Far Eastern Quarterly 139 (1948).

24. G. Warp, *In Our Image and Likeness,* 42 National Municipal Review 176 (1957).

25. J. Spae, *Neighborhood Associations: A Catholic Way for Japan* (1956).

26. Beardsley et al., *supra* note 18, at 351.

27. Quoted in Steiner, *supra* note 2, at 238. For viewpoints of official American critics, see 1 Government Section GHQ, in SCAP, *Political Reorientation of Japan* (1949), at 284-88; J. Masland, *Neighborhood Associations in Japan*, 15 Far Eastern Survey 355 (1948), see also R. Ward, *Socio-Political Role of the Boraka in Japan*, 45 American Political Science Review 1025 (1957). For the views of Japanese critics, see E. Isomura, et al., *Recent Trends of Urban Sociology in Japan*, 10 Sociological Review Monograph 127-50 (1966).

28. Steiner, *supra* note 2, at 502, n.19.

29. E. Ben-Ari, *Changing Japanese Suburbia* (1991), at 39, 42. See *id.* at 49 for a listing of no fewer than a dozen city-affiliated associations in a typical neighborhood.

30. Steiner, *supra* note 2, at 75.

31. *Id.* at 221.

32. Fukutake, *supra* note 1, at 115, 117.

33. M. Keiichi, *Citizen Participation in Historical Perspective* in *Authority and the Individual in Japan* (J. Koschman ed. 1978), at 182.

34. D. Bayley, *Forces of Order: Police Behavior in Japan and the United States* (1973), at 94.

35. *Id.* See W. Ames, *Police and Community in Japan* (1981), at 42.

36. Steiner, *supra* note 2, at 217.

37. Fukutake, *supra* note 1, at 137.

38. See W. Clifford, *Crime Control in Japan* (1976), describing the displacement of Police Law 196 of 1947 by Police Law 162 of 1954 and the extinction of the preexisting 1,600 municipal police forces with the acquiescence of the Occupation authorities concerned with reinforcing controls against subversion.

39. K. Von Wolforen, *The Enigma of Japanese Power* (1989), ch. 7 n.5, citing S. Garon, *The Imperial Bureaucracy and Labor Policy in Post-war Japan*, Journal of Asian Studies 1984), at 442.

40. W. Ames, *supra* note 35, at 135.

41. *Id.* at 23.

42. Bayley, *supra* note 34, at 75.

43. *Id.* at 180.

44. *Id.* at 25.

45. *Id.* at 84.

46. *Id.* at 72.

47. D. Westey, *The Emulation of Western Organizations in Meiji Japan: The Case of the Paris Prefecture of Police*, 1982 Journal of Japanese Studies (1982), at 315.

48. *Id.* at 73, 74.

49. *Id.* at 228.

50. *Id.* at 83.

51. *Id.* at 228.

52. Clifford, *supra* note 38, at 109.

53. W. Ames, *supra* note 35.

54. Bayley, *supra* note 34, at 101.

55. *Id.* at 156.

56. T. Fukutake, *supra* note 1, at 146-47. The figures given are for 1978; the 1973 figures were 35% and 59%. On the contemporary revival of traditional associations for purposes such as pesticide application, alley lighting, emergency care, funeral aid, recycling and volunteer fire-fighting, see T. Bestor, *Tradition and Japanese Social Organization: Institutional Development in a Tokyo Neighborhood*, 24 Ethnology 121 (1985).

57. Bayley, *supra* note 34, at 195, 198.

58. Clifford, *supra* note 38, at 176.

59. C. Black et al., *The Modernization of Japan and Russia* (1975), at 49.

60. *Id.* at 215.

61. Fukutake, *supra* note 1, at 216-17. See also E. Norbeck, *Japanese Common Interest Associations in Cross-Cultural Perspective*, 1 Journal of Voluntary Action Scholars 38 (1972).

62. Ben-Ari, *supra* note 29, at 94, 119.

63. See *id.*, at 128; T. Campbell, *The Old People Boom and Japanese Policymaking*, 5 Journal of Japanese Studies 321 (1974); A. Ernst, *A Segmented Welfare State*, 138 Journal of Institutional and Theoretical Economics 545 (1982).

64. See Ben-Ari, *supra* note 29, at 147-60. *Id.* at 165. See S. Linhart, *The Search for Meaning in Old Age, The Japanese Case*, 12 International Congress of Gerontology (1981).

65. Ben-Ari, *supra* note 29, at 12-13.

66. Van Wolferen, *supra* note 39, ch. 7 n.14.

67. W. Dore, *City Life in Japan* (1958), at 285.

68. D. Maeda, *Decline of Family Love and the Development of Public Services*, in *An Aging World: Dilemmas and Challenges for Law and Social Policy* (J. Eekelaar et al. eds. 1989), at 313.

69. W. Coaldrake, *The Architecture of Reality: Trends in Japanese Housing 1985-89*, Japan Architect, October 1989, at 61, 66. A survey in Osaka in 1987 found that 32% of families lived with their aging parents, while 53% stated they would like to do so if this were possible.

70. Dore, *supra* note 67, at 287.

Conclusions

This inquiry was inspired viscerally by the fact that the author has spent nearly all his life in four more-than-ordinarily-troubled American cities, New York, Chicago, Washington, and Baltimore, and intellectually by what seemed to the author the extraordinary growth of residential community associations, historic, special, and business improvement districts in the United States over the last two decades. The residential community association had its roots in the federal mortgage lending regulations, whose authors never dreamed that they were composing constitutions for American suburban society. The growth in number and function of these institutions has been nationwide but has been particularly marked in California in the wake of the fiscal collapse of local government brought on by the tax revolt of the 1980s.

With respect to absolute and relative social and economic deprivations and alienation from the community, "one of the crucial elements in the destructive-ness of both problems is the fact that the victims no longer perceive a role for themselves in their solution--they become spectators of their own humiliation."[1] Where housing regulations segregate economic classes and generations, and residential and commercial land uses, where complexes are devoid of stores, meeting places, day care centers, organizations for the aged, market stalls, playgrounds, pubs and restaurants, localized police protection, and tenant associations, it is too soon to ascribe their social problems primarily to lack of employment opportunities or income transfers. Nor is it likely that a political majority will accede to massive income transfers: "[A]ll modern liberal welfare states increasingly transfer funds, not from rich to poor, but to the middle classes. Those who most need help get very little of it."[2]

The American economy was in no small measure built by immigrant groups, many with limited skills, who made their own economic opportunities in less favorable circumstances in terms of housing quality, health care, infrastructure, and income support: One may instance the gardeners and laundrymen of the West Coast, the construction workers and merchants of the East, and, perhaps tomorrow, the better organized providers of home maintenance, child care, retail delivery, demand-response transportation, and restaurant services required by a changing economy in which women have entered the workforce in large numbers.   Unless it is part of the American national agenda to shatter with bombs the industry of all other developed and developing nations, the exceptional conditions of the 1950s are not going to return, for American inner-city dwellers or for any one else.   The crisis of the inner cities is not fundamentally due to the inability of their residents to obtain lifelong unskilled jobs with indexed pensions at the local union hall; to suggest that it is, is in truth a counsel of despair.

   In recent years, a great deal has been written, some of it by this writer, about problems of family breakdown in the inner cities.   The effort to ascribe these problems primarily to lack of opportunities for male wage earners is in the end also unconvincing; this problem also has social and cultural as well as economic roots, in the design of the welfare state, in the politically aided decline of religious institutions, and in modern mass communications and the use to which they are put.   The sexual emancipation, self-realization, and women's liberation that have enriched the lives of at least some of the comfortable and prosperous have had different effects when communicated to more vulnerable groups, for reasons which would have been well understood by Adam Smith:

In every civilized society, in every society where the distinction of ranks has once been completely established, there have been always two different schemes or systems of morality current at the same time; of which the one may be called the strict or austere; the other the liberal, or, if you will, the loose system.   The former is generally admired and revered by the common people; the latter is commonly more esteemed and adopted by what are called people of fashion.   The degree of disapprobation with which we ought to mark the vices of levity, the vices which are apt to arise from great prosperity, and from the excess of gaiety and good humour, seems to constitute the principal distinction between those two opposite schemes or systems.   In the liberal or loose system, luxury, wanton and even disorderly mirth, the pursuit of pleasure to some degree of intemperance, the breach of chastity, at least in one of the two sexes, provided they are not accompanied with gross indecency, and do not lead to falsehood or injustice, are generally treated with a good deal of indulgence, and are easily either excused or pardoned altogether.   In the austere system, on the contrary, those excesses are regarded with the utmost abhorrence and detestation.   The vices of levity are always ruinous to the common people, and a single week's thoughtlessness and dissipation is often sufficient to undo a poor workman for ever, and to drive him through despair upon committing the most enormous crimes. The wiser and better sort of the common people, therefore, have always the utmost abhorrence and detestation for such excesses, which their experience tells them are so immediately fatal to people of their condition.   The disorder and extravagance of several years, on the contrary, will not always ruin a man of fashion, and people of that rank are very apt to consider the power of indulging in some degree of excess as one of the advantages of their fortune, and the liberty of doing so without censure or reproach, as one of the privileges which belong to their station. In people of their own station, therefore, they regard such excesses with but a small degree of disapprobation, and censure them either very slightly or not at all.

Almost all religious sects have begun among the common people, from whom they have generally drawn their earliest, as well as their most numerous proselytes. The austere system of morality has, accordingly, been adopted by those sects almost constantly, or with very few exceptions; for there have been some. It was the system by which they could best recommend themselves to that order of people to whom they first proposed their plan of reformation upon what had been before established . . . .

A man of rank and fortune is by his station the distinguished member of a great society, who attend to every part of his conduct, and who thereby oblige him to attend to every part of it himself. His authority and consideration depend very much upon the respect which this society bears to him. He dare not do any thing which would disgrace or discredit him in it, and he is obliged to a very strict observation of that species of morals, whether liberal or austere, which the general consent of this society prescribes to persons of his rank and fortune. A man of low condition, on the contrary, is far from being a distinguished member of any great society. While he remains in a country village his conduct may be attended to, and he may be obliged to attend to it himself. In this situation, and in this situation only, he may have what is called character to lose. But as soon as he comes into a great city, he is sunk in obscurity and darkness. His conduct is observed and attended to by nobody, and he is therefore very likely to neglect it himself, and to abandon himself to every sort of low profligacy and vice. He never emerges so effectually from his obscurity, his conduct never excites so much the attention of any respectable society, as by his becoming the member of a small religious sect. He from that moment acquires a degree of consideration which he never had before. All his brother sectaries are, for the credit of the sect, interested to observe his conduct, and, if he gives occasion to any scandal, if he deviates very much from those austere morals which they almost always require of one another, to punish him by what is expulsion or excommunication from the sect. In little religious sects, accordingly, the morals of the common people have been almost always remarkably regular and orderly; generally much more so than in the established church. The morals of those little sects, indeed, have frequently been rather disagreeably rigorous and unsocial.[3]

This view as to the significance of religious institutions, shared by many of the framers of the American Constitution, calls into question many modern assumptions as to the relation between religious institutions and modernity. As Page Smith noted in his study of American towns: "Here was the paradox: The covenanted community, remarkably stable and unshakably conservative, produced outwardly-propelled, inner-directed individuals capable of the most startling innovation and the most revolutionary change, carried through in the name of the ancient values of the town."[4]

Economics, and more particularly economic education, and adjustment of welfare systems may supply the answer to some of the present difficulties, but for much of the rest, we must look to Smith's "sects" and, as the present work suggests, also to his "villages."

This preliminary explanation of the use of small-scale "governments" is an effort to sketch both benefits to be obtained and hazards to be avoided. Exploration of the history of residential associations in the United States, communes in France, and parish councils in England reveals that, contrary to the received belief about the competency of small units, even very small entities have the capacity to meet local needs by contracting out for service provision. At a time when just that policy is increasingly the practice of national governments in England, Germany, and the United States, demands for the rationalization of small units appear misplaced.

EDUCATION

Indeed, in England, Australia, New Zealand and parts of the United States, strenuous efforts are being made to undo the enforced consolidation of schools and school districts that was once an assured part of any "reform" agenda. In education, at least, bureaucratic competence has reached and exceeded its limits, and closed shops, teachers' unions, and the escalation of costs at a rate exceeding both inflation and any discernible improvement in schools have produced the reaction that so many deplore.

COMMUNITY CARE

Similarly, the increase in the demands on government presented by the very old and the very young make new approaches imperative. The rising elderly population cannot be cared for in the government-supported nursing homes such as those fortuitously called into existence by the Medicaid program in the United States, consistent with any notion of fiscal responsibility. Nor can the young children of the increasing number of two-earner families also be cared for in state institutions--institutions whose ability to effectively teach older children is already doubtful. If these problems are to be met, measures to foster mutual aid, and to end the segregation of the generations, so as to allow working parents to look after their elderly, and the elderly to assist in the care of the young, are needed.

In the housing complexes of the deprived, child care is the one commodity in potential oversupply. In that connection, it is not without significance that Germany, Japan, and England have provided fiscal incentives for the private creation of second units in existing homes, and that Japan and some American and Canadian subdivisions have begun to relax land use restrictions against the creation of such units by property owners. The systematic effort in both Japan and Russia to enlist the aid of the elderly in mutual care and care of the young and in England to organize play groups also has lessons to teach, as does the increasing importance in British social policy toward the aged of what is loosely and sometimes vaguely referred to as "community care."

Much has been said, by Bertrand Russell, H. G. Wells, and others, of the irrelevance of the neighborhood unit in a society in which employed persons have many economic and other interests outside the neighborhood, but it cannot be denied that the very old, the very young, and their caretakers are to a considerable extent rooted there. Although these are not the most politically articulate classes, they and the cause of local area organization, deserve more attention than they have received.

TRAFFIC LIMITATION

In Western Europe at least, measures are beginning to be taken to deal with the socially destructive effects of automobile use, by the creation with local assent of large pedestrian zones in central cities in an effort to preserve their character. Similar impulses, less clearly associated with identification of the automobile as a major source of urban blight, drive the historic preservation movement in England, France, and America. All these schemes generally involve the creation or recognition of small formal or informal districts of governance.

Perhaps even more important, there has been recognition in Western Europe and in scattered places in the United States of the problems caused by the overbuilding of urban streets in residential neighborhoods, particularly those laid out on the grid pattern so fashionable in the early years of this century. Measures are increasingly being taken following the suggestions of Jacobs, Mumford, and others to close off the ends of streets so as to create artificial squares and cul-de-sacs, or to install traffic calming devices so as to allow both the street and associated sidewalks to be reclaimed for recreational use. Both these sets of devices eliminate the waste of paved land, and both call into existence formal (as in Holland and St. Louis) or informal communities of street abutters to govern the partially privatized streets.

Of a piece with these efforts are suggestions for the reconfiguration of existing block patterns, in both the cities and their suburbs. In the cities, street closings and the creation of "superblocks" to facilitate urban renewal projects, together with measures to reduce the ability of individual property owners to object to development at established densities, have been suggested, and there has been some revived interest in devices such as the Lex Adickes for consolidation of plats in Germany and in special benefit assessments in the United States.

SOCIAL ORGANIZATION OF HOUSING PROJECTS

Governments in all the countries examined have belatedly recognized the need for greater interest in the social organization of public housing--housing usually occupied by the most dependent and susceptible groups in the community. Dissatisfaction with high-rise units as family residences is now virtually universal, save perhaps in Russia where units have been rendered "liveable" through stringent measures of social control and transit linkages with city centers. With respect to low-rise units, it is increasingly appreciated that "architectural determinism" is not enough and that even the best-planned mixed-use communities have failed to reach their potential where some form of community governance is not provided.

COMMUNITY LAW ENFORCEMENT

Even in the realm of law enforcement, there is detectable in Western countries renewed interest in devices resembling the community-based law enforcement that prevailed in the 600 years following enactment of the Statute of Winchester in 1285. In the United States and England, and to some extent in Germany, neighborhood watch organizations have proliferated, and there has been rising interest in decentralization of police functions. The slightly increased use of wanted posters and comparable radio and television programs represents a return to the "hue and cry" in the sense of Henry Fielding's crime pursuit circulars, if not in the medieval sense of hot pursuit. Community crime prevention campaigns directed at "target hardening" are increasingly common.

These have been, in Western countries, largely unconscious tendencies, and many, if not most, of them have gained acceptability not as impositions of community governance but as expressions of private property rights. Thus, traffic calming increases the property owner's dominion over the street, residential community associations confer on him power over common areas, tenants' associations and neighborhood watch programs are perceived as measures for the protection of property, and the ability to reconfigure houses and yards and to appoint governors of schools likewise gain acceptance as additions to private rights.

THE PERILS OF NEIGHBORHOOD

This book has sought to render these processes more self-conscious. The democratic nations concerned have been surveyed because many of their practices are adaptable to each other's circumstances. The Russian and Chinese experience is surveyed less for this reason than for others. Certainly there are elements of

Soviet and Chinese practice that there is no reason to shrink from adopting--the efforts to mobilize the elderly for mutual aid and care of the young, and perhaps the Russian practice of paroling offenders to collective entities. But there are other elements of Chinese and Soviet practice that Westerners regard with instinctive revulsion and that have rendered the whole notion of small-neighborhood governance suspect. The chapters have made explicit what these features are: identity checks; residency controls; the governmental appointment, rather than democratic election, of neighborhood officers; neighborhood adjudication of offenses; and the creation of networks of police informers. "The point of the Soviet community organizational effort," Theodore Friedgut has observed, "is to make your regime your neighbor by having your neighbor represent your regime."[5]

In addition to the Soviet and Chinese examples, the abuse of the "neighborhood" concept by the American and British left in the 1960s has not fostered intelligent interest in its possibilities. Demands for "participatory democracy" contemplated only a certain kind of participation, by participants of a certain political stripe. As was observed in an historical dictionary of American community organizations published in 1986:

Organization to provide residents control over neighborhood operations in 1910 meant creating a healthier urban community by strengthening one of its constituent parts. In the 1980s, the emphasis is inner-directed. Little concern exists for the larger urban community. . . . After 1920 . . . community organization increasingly focussed on strategies of advocacy and competition for scarce resources, rather than on fostering a civic consciousness that identified with, yet transcended the local community and incorporated it into the whole of the American experience.[6]

Because the youth of the 1960s were, in George Kennan's words, "rebels without a program" whose agenda was not institutional but consisted of claims on the national government and demands for unchecked private behavior, their movement left little positive residue. The formless nature of the demands together with the fact that their only potential allies in northern countries were bureaucracies and labor organizations heavily wedded to existing bureaucratic institutions further operated to vitiate them. Significantly, it was only in France, where the leading party of the Left was not wedded to the trade unions and where there were also important anarchist and Catholic intellectual traditions emphasizing subsidiarity that important change took place. Decentralization in Britain, the United States, and West Germany, when it occurred, was informed by many of the same political impulses, but took the form of privatization and reliance on market institutions.

The aspiration, through privatization, to create a property-owning democracy is not to be despised, as was noted by Richard Pipes in the quotation included in the Russian chapter. "It is only through the participation of the unknown many in the responsibilities and determinations of business," Mr. Justice Brandeis observed, "that Americans can secure the moral and intellectual development essential to the maintenance of liberty."[7] As applied to migrants at the bottom of society, and to groups such as dependent unemployed women, such a policy is not by itself enough. Abhorrent though we find the techniques of total mobilization of totalitarian states, the problems that they addressed were quite real. As the family disintegration promoted by recent liberation movements proceeds, accompanied by ever-greater laissez-faire and instability of employment in the economic marketplace, the problems of the underclass are becoming the problems of society generally, and particularly of its young.

The suburban woman of the 1950s, Lewis Mumford once observed, "approximated, in modern terms, conditions required for citizenship in the Greek polis: leisure, detachment from base occupations, concern for public goods."[8] An equally sanguine but diametrically opposed commentator described the ensuing "moral order of the suburb" as constituting the wave of the future for all communities:

The suburbs lack social cohesion but they are free of strife. They are, so to speak, disorganized and orderly at the same time. . . . The most apparently disintegrating tendencies of modern life actually breed a harmonious social order all their own. . . . [I]t appears that more and more people live in an environment characterized by transiency and fragmentation of social networks, along with spatial separation, privacy, and insulation from strangers. . . . Moral minimalization should become an ever more pervasive feature of modern life . . . a study in the moral order of the future.[9]

It may be doubted, however, whether this "moral order" can survive the collapse of the nuclear family at its base. At least some of the self-conscious methods of social control pursued by the Japanese in recent years, including the promotion of a revived extended family and the neighborhood organization of the elderly, thus warrant consideration.

THE POSITIVE CASE FOR NEIGHBORHOOD INSTITUTIONS

The case for enhanced and formalized neighborhood governance made here has been made in somber and negative terms: Institutions are needed to replace or supplement other social controls. There is no intention, however, to neglect the positive case for participatory institutions.

People of the West are accustomed to thinking of the Athenian Assembly, a body meeting regularly ten times a year, as the paradigm of direct democracy. While this body included the whole population of male citizens, this has been characterized as "rather a political myth than a form of government."[10] The basis of the Athenian local government under the constitution of Cleisthenes (507 B.C.) was the "deme," of which there were perhaps a hundred. Membership in these was hereditary.[11]   Their functions included the election of officers, the management of parish lands, the conduct of festivals, judicial power, but only in a limited number of specially referred local cases, maintenance of the register of citizenship and, most important, the raising of taxes and the designation of citizens to perform the work of the government.[12]   Since the resident adult citizen population was estimated at from 35,000 to 44,000,[13] the typical deme had a size roughly equivalent to that of today's typical community association.

The ideal sought was that of Pericles's funeral oration: "We alone regard a man who takes no interest in public affairs, not as a harmless, but as a useless character; and if few of us are originators, we are all sound judges of policy."[14] This concern animated the political writings of both Plato and Aristotle. It has been said that "the failure of the city-state is drawn like a sharp line across the history of political thought. . . . [M]en had to learn to live alone as they had never done, and they had to learn to live together in a new form of social union much larger and more impersonal than the city-state."[15]   Participation as a central concern of political theory in the West did not make its reappearance until the time of Rousseau.

Rousseau's conception of the general will has often and justly been described as a progenitor of totalitarianism.[16]   But although this conception has been projected onto a national stage, it is clear that Rousseau had in mind the general will of direct assemblies of very small size:

In the first place, the State must be sufficiently small to make it possible to call the whole people together without difficulty, and each citizen must be in a position to know all his neighbors. In the second place, manners must be so simple that business will be kept to a minimum and thorny questions avoided. There should be, too, considerable equality in fortune and in rank, for otherwise there will not long be equality in rights and authority. Finally there must be little or no luxury, because either it is the product of wealth or its makes wealth necessary. It corrupts both the rich and the poor, the rich through their possessions, the poor through their lust to possess.[17]

Jeffersonian proposals for ward government, elaborated in a series of letters and in his autobiographical writings,[18] were consciously proposals for local government, not government of a total society. Such governments could exist only within "very narrow limits of space and population."[19]   The Jeffersonian ward was to be rural in character, was to have four elected officers, a warden, a justice of the peace, a constable, and a captain of militia; and was to discharge a limited catalogue of functions, including the administration of local justice, care of the poor, elementary education, raising of the militia, selection of jurors, and conduct of elections.[20]   Although, for reasons the present writer has outlined elsewhere, the justice of the peace system never took proper root in America[21] and the external threats facing the country do not require a highly prepared local militia,[22] the recent reaction against overprofessionalization of both the schools and the police[23] and the continuing use of small election districts give the rest of the Jeffersonian project continuing pertinence.

Mill likewise upheld the prerogatives of local government, though confining its scope to "the administration of the poor laws, sanitary regulations," "the paving, lighting and cleaning of the streets of a town and in ordinary circumstances the draining of its houses."[24] Once again, the justification was participation:

Though individuals may not do the particular thing so well, on the average, as the officers of government, it is nevertheless desirable that it should be done by them, rather than by the government, as a means to their own mental education. . . . These are not questions of liberty, and are connected with that subject only by remote tendencies, but they are questions of development . . . in truth, the peculiar training of a citizen; the practical part of the political education of a free people, taking them out of the narrow circle of personal and family selfishness and accustoming them to the comprehension of joint interests, the management of joint concerns--habituating them to act from public or semi-public motives and guide their conduct by aims which unite instead of isolating them from one another. Without these habits and powers, a free constitution can neither be worked nor preserved; as is amplified by the too-often transitory political freedom in countries where it does not rest on a basis of local liberties.[25]

Similarly, de Tocqueville stressed the significance of local against central government that "every day renders the exercise of the free agency of men less frequent."[26] More contemporary writers have echoed similar themes. The limitations of a purely market-driven society are noted by sympathetic critics such as Schumpeter and Niebuhr. Schumpeter stated, "The capitalist order rests on props made of extra-capitalist patterns of behavior which at the same time it is bound to destroy."[27] Niebuhr stated, "Life requires a more organic and mutual form than bourgeois democracy provides for it; but the social substance of life is richer and more various and has greater depths and tensions than are envisaged in the Marxist dream of social harmony."[28]

The advent of modern totalitarianism led to a postwar reaction in favor of ideals of community and mediating institutions. The postwar critics of an undifferentiated suburbia, most notably William H. Whyte, Jr., a noted zoning reformer, [29] and David Riesman, with his appeal for utopian thinking,[30] sounded these themes: "Riesman and Whyte have been pointing in their recent jeremiads to an organization society: a self-defeating attempt by an atomizing society to reproduce order by uniformity, whom suddenly . . . society becomes aware that its 'separatenesses' are proliferating at a geometric rate."[31]

The latter day Marxists, with their references to alienation in a capitalist order, sounded similar themes, albeit less constructively. Thus, C. Wright Mills said that "they feel that they live in a time of big decisions; they know that they are not making any."[32] Those in Europe preparing plans for reconstruction after the war saw more clearly. Thus, Simone Weil, in her prospectus for de Gaulle, stated:

[T]he State has morally killed everything, territorially speaking, smaller than itself. . . . It is only possible partially to repair the past and this can only be done through a recognized local and regional life receiving the unreserved encouragement of the authorities within the setting of the French nation . . . .

It is necessary that a man should often have to take decisions in matters great or small affecting interests that are distinct from his own, but in regard to which he feels a personal concern.

. . . [A] flourishing local and regional life ought to furnish whoever is able to take advantage of it with the opportunity to command at certain periods of his life.[33]

In her commentary *On Revolution*, Hannah Arendt noted "the regular emergence, during the course of revolution of a new form of government that resembled in an amazing fashion Jefferson's ward system and seemed to repeat, under no matter what circumstances, the revolutionary societies and municipal councils which had spread all over France after 1789."[34]

If we leave aside the February Revolution of 1848 in Paris . . . the main dates of appearance of these organs of action and germs of a new state are the following: the year 1870, when the French capital under siege by the Prussian army "spontaneously reorganized itself into a miniature federal body" . . . the year 1905, when the wave of spontaneous strikes in Russia developed a political leadership of its own . . . The February Revolution of 1917 in Russia . . . the years 1918 and 1919 in Germany, when, after the defeat of the army, soldiers and workers in open rebellion constituted themselves into Arbeiter and Soldatenrate. . . . [T]he last date, finally, is the autumn of 1956, when the Hungarian Revolution from its very beginning produced the council system anew in Budapest.[35]

These revolutionary councils or Jefferson's "ward republics" were for Arendt "the best instruments . . . for breaking up the modern mass society, with its dangerous tendency toward the formation of pseudo-political mass movements, or rather, the best, the most natural way for interspersing it at the grass roots with an "elite" that is chosen by no one but constitutes itself."[36] "It was nothing more or less than this hope of the modern egalitarian society to become a 'participator' in public affairs, that was buried in the disasters of twentieth-century revolutions."[37] The temporary nature of these structures, however, like those of wartime, may supply the strongest argument against Arendt's thesis: people, as they are, will not voluntarily live for long in conditions of total civic mobilization.

Robert Nisbet, in the most notable postwar essay on these problems, observed:

One thinks of the innumerable suburbs that have sprung up since the Second World War
. . . where there is little more sense of community than there is in the housing project.
How could this be? Community is the product of people working together on problems,
of autonomous and collective fulfillment of internal objectives, and of the experience of
living under codes of authority which have been set in large degree by the persons
involved. But what we get in many sections of the country is a kind of suburban horde.
There is no community because there are no common problems, functions and authority.
. . . [U]nder a kind of "rotten borough" system, effective control is vested elsewhere--in
boards, councils, and offices of counties, districts or adjacent cities.[38]

More recently David Popenoe has observed, "Why bemoan the decline of the
neighborhood unit? Because the needs and functions it once served are still
highly important. These include mutual aid, sociability and friendship, [and] the
socialization of children.[39] "Following the European lead, the United States
should make a much greater effort to achieve a rearrangement of local
government jurisdictions around viable social entities. . . . [s]ome have
suggested clustering of several hundred or more households, enough to make up
a neighborhood primary school."[40] Similarly, sociologist Peter Berger has
appealed for "[z]oning and housing policies that work with rather than against
existing communities and for life styles (always with the proviso that such
policies are not racially exclusive and do not infringe on the rights of individuals). . . . Decentralization and community control of some functions of
municipal government (including law enforcement and health delivery).[41]"
    We may recall in this context the warning that

among the units most needed in the world as it has been evolving lie several at the
extremes. . . . At the same time that the transnational units will increase the capacity
of the system to handle critical problems, and thus the collective effectiveness of a body
of citizens, transnational units will also increase the ineffectuality and powerlessness of
the individual citizen.[42]

The typical community association, unlike the unwisely reapportioned electorial
district, has natural boundaries, not the local government boundaries, satirized by
Wells, "determined by mapping out the wanderings of an intoxicated excursionist."[43] It is undoubtedly true, as critics of overuse of the association model have
noted, that "an individualistic consumer model cannot prepare people adequately
to govern a CID [Community Improvement District]."[44] "The dominant
individualist trend of American thought makes it difficult for a citizen without
special education or training in community organization to conceive of the
possibility of creating a community."[45] In addition, "actual neighborhoods
. . . attract individuals who have no such prior attachment or common goals,
who may not want to make the commitment to any group, or to a new group and
who are also, once established, less able to leave."[46]

But it also remains true that man is a social animal and that much of what community associations can do responds to felt needs, to service delivery failures, and to zoning overregulation by higher levels of government and that the impulse toward participation, if not satisfied at the community level, may take other, more malign forms:

The demand for participatory democracy and the acceptance of supervised efforts at personal transparency ("encounter groups" and the like) seem to be on the increase as autonomy and independence decline. It is possible that processes very different from those envisaged by either Marx or Rousseau are present in the modern world . . . [T]he nature and quality and significance of the craving for participation may go beyond what they had in mind.[47]

In recent years we have seen the development of several types of "pseudo-communities," groups of individuals who share some critical problem of social adjustment or personal malaise . . . It is certainly clear that pseudo-communities are more problematical and unstable than the type of community experience represented by the American small town."[48]

Neighborhood association constitutes a reaction against the rationalization of local government in the progressive era, lending to the prophecy that "the wave of reform after the one now in progress will rally under a banner of earlier days: take administration out of politics and politics out of administration."[49] "Power . . . can take only two organizational forms, centralized or decentralized, and reform . . . amounts to an oscillation from one to the other. The change itself amounts to a reform. . . . But in political organization this . . . has not, ordinarily, taken place."[50]

Thus, considerations both large and small may support the enhancement of community associations.

We will need experiments as well as great debates. . . . We need to give ordinary men a renewed connection with the political action of their society. Whether they customarily make use of that connection or not, it should exist, so that when the occasions arise . . . they can make their will felt.[51]

FEMINISM AND NEIGHBORHOOD

In addition to the need for social control and for political participation, dramatic demographic changes may support a new look at neighborhood institutions, a point made by many feminist writers.[52] It has been noted that during the four decades ending in 1980, 80.4 million new dwelling units were built in the United States, of which 53.9 million were single-family detached units.[53] This housing stock is increasingly ill-adapted to a population in which there are more single people living alone,[54] the age of marriage is delayed,[55] average family size is sharply declining,[56] there are an increased number of families headed by women as a result of both increases in unwed motherhood[57] and in the divorce rate,[58] and the percentage of elderly women living with relatives has sharply declined.[59] This has led Dolores Hayden, author of the most comprehensive critique from this perspective, to forecast that "over two or three decades most of the single-family housing stock and most of the R-1 neighborhoods will change to reflect the basic demographic shifts the U.S. faces."[60]

The single-family suburb from which mixed uses are excluded is especially dysfunctional for female-headed families. The common caricature is of a harassed head of family who is compelled by zoning to live in a detached house, because no other housing is available; who is required to commute to a distant office (zoned out of the neighborhood); to drive long distances for even the simplest household purchases (as a result of the exclusion of convenience stores); to travel further long distances to visit parents (as a result of the exclusion of apartments, including accessory apartments); and then, when these daily duties are discharged, who is expected to mow an unwanted lawn. These grievances have led to proposals for zoning change for existing neighborhoods.

Zoning has never acknowledged that most industrial activities have lost obnoxious qualities; it has, on the contrary, steadily deepened and refined its separatist tendencies. . . . [E]veryone's journey for purposes of shopping or working or engaging in any other activities is significantly lengthened. . . . [It is a] destroyer of urbane qualities and of urban activities, by making human communication as difficult as possible.[61]

"The adaptation of suburban house forms to new uses is as inevitable as was the adaptation of brick row houses and brownstones and the introduction of mixed uses, higher densities and new building types that accompanied it."[62] The Hayden proposals call for the legalization of accessory apartments but only where "they comply with a neighborhood improvement plan [and] pay for additional amenities."[63] Other proposals presupposing an expanded role for neighborhood governance include "making vacant lots into parks and playgrounds . . . babysitting co-ops and car pools . . . recycling garage sales, small licensed day care providers."[64]

These proposals are tendered in recognition of the fact that "most employed adults in the United States are not interested in moving toward communal groups,[65] nor are they interested in having new bureaucracies run family life."[66] Thus, there is a call for legal remodeling "within the context of replanned blocks"[67] and in addition to legalization of accessory apartments, subdivision of existing homes is sought: "If they could . . . become co-owners of private spaces within these parents' homes rather than theirs, it might add to the attraction of living in a separate apartment in the same dwelling."[68]

Other writers have likewise condemned single-family zoning as having "effectively broken up . . . older patterns of mutual support and stratified the population by, among other things, age and stage in the family cycle."[69] The absence of mixed uses has also been blamed for problems in the upbringing of the young.[70]

SOME CONCRETE SUGGESTIONS

What are the concrete implications of all this to those who welcome "community" but fear totalitarianism; who desire to foster mechanisms of cooperation while neither wishing nor expecting democratic systems to behave as if in a state of total mobilization for revolution or war; who seek workable social improvement and forswear utopian schemes? Perhaps the following may serve as a summary.

1. Persons abutting streets in large cities should be encouraged but not required to form street associations, with authority to petition for calming devices or cul-de-sac treatment and to collect modest taxes or dues.

A suitable pattern may be found in the developing law relating to historic and special districts and in the 1985 proposals of the U.S. Advisory Commission on Intergovernmental Relations allowing districts with their own governing bodies to be created on petition with supermajority but not unanimous approval. Since states enacting such statutes for existing neighborhoods would be writing on a substantially clean slate, one-man/one-vote voting could be provided in place of a property owners' franchise. The resulting associations would be subject to constitutional constraints that do not bind owner-created associations and that might preclude some membership restrictions and aesthetic controls impairing existing interests; however, a wide scope of activity could still be made available to them. Indeed, tax sharing would be feasible, as is probably not the case with associations organized on the basis of a property owners' franchise.

2. Street closings, the reconfiguration of small blocks into superblocks for redevelopment purposes, and the use of vacant land to create squares are appropriate urban strategies.

3. Community, street, and block associations should be empowered by rule to waive zoning restrictions against mixed uses, day care centers, and accessory apartments, subject to safeguards against external effects.

4. In suburban areas not possessing community associations, block associations should be fostered. An expeditious means should be provided to permit residents by agreement to reconfigure the interior of blocks.

5. Clubs and mutual aid groups for the aged should be fostered at the block and street level, and services to the aged should be delivered at this level.

6. There should be continued development of volunteer, noncompulsory neighborhood watch organizations, greater publicity for criminal convictions (as opposed to offenses), and enhanced use of compendia of wanted circulars and crime prevention suggestions on the eighteenth century model.

7. Use of block or street associations as parole agents or agents to discharge other social service functions might be permitted where associations accept this responsibility.

8. The statute governing street and block associations should require election of officers and supermajority votes for the assumption of new functions.

9. Responsibilities (and associated revenues) for street and park maintenance or improvement should be delegated to associations willing to accept them where external effects will not result.

10. Tenants' associations with the power to manage common areas and a portion of maintenance budgets should be freely created in public projects.

11. No judicial functions or powers should be attempted to be delegated, other than the power to collect dues and assessments.

12. In general, activities in aid of law enforcement should be limited to reporting observed offenses. There should be no listings of residents given to the police, home inspections, or actions of like character.

13. Election precinct boundaries should be conformed to those of associations.

14. Formal liaison committees with associations in their area should be established by elementary schools.

15. Associations should be given dispensations from sales, admissions and amusement taxes and related licensing and reporting requirements.

16. Associations acting by supermajority votes should be given defined powers to impose regulations relating to such matters as parking, aesthetics (with grandfathering of preexisting uses) and juvenile curfews enforced by public authority.

17. Associations electing to operate day care centers should receive the same public assistance and subsidies as other licensees.

18. These principles likewise should apply to existing subdivisions, such as villages, communes, or parishes.

CONCLUSION

It may be doubted that there is much to fear from these limited delegations. "Local government may be legitimized by factors unlike those that legitimize government on a larger scale . . . a combination of Hirschman's elements: voice in the ability to participate in decisions . . . and exit in the parties' ultimate ability to withdraw and go elsewhere."[71]

In the language of Henry Simons, "[e]xtensive local socialization need not be incompatible with, or very dangerous to, a free society. Local bodies are themselves largely voluntary associations; people have much freedom to choose and to move among them; they are substantially competitive and, even if permitted to do so, rarely could much restrain trade."[72] Delegation of powers to the neighborhood level thus appeals alike to "the strong opposite biases in favor of either exit or voice which come almost naturally to the economist and political scientist respectively."[73]

Literal "exit" is not the only nonpolitical limitation on oppressive regulations, since these will have effects on perceived desirability of neighborhoods and on property values, a subject to which property owners are keenly sensitive.

It was, indeed, a strong devotee of free markets, Hayek, who told us:

[T]o re-entrust the management of most service activities of government to smaller units would probably lead to the revival of a communal spirit which has largely been suffocated by centralization. The widely felt inhumanity of the modern society is not so much the result of the impersonal character of the economic process, in which modern man of necessity works largely for aims of which he is ignorant, but of the fact that political centralization has largely deprived him of the chance to have a say in shaping the environment which he knows.[74]

This view as to government, if not the economy, is echoed in the classic Catholic statement of the principle of subsidiarity (implicitly endorsed in the famous section 3[b] of the Treaty of Maastricht) contained in Pius XI's *Quadrigesimo Anno* (1931):

Just as it is wrong to withdraw from the individual and to commit to the community at large what private enterprise and endeavor can accomplish, so it is likewise unjust and a gravely harmful disturbance of right order to turn over to a greater society of higher rank functions and services which can be performed by lesser bodies on a lower plane. For a social undertaking of any sort, by its very nature, ought to aid the members of the body social, but never to destroy and absorb them.[75]

The case for artificial stimulation of new entities rests on the premise stated by a distinguished contemporary political scientist that "participants themselves cannot create the institution, for the same reason that they need it in the first place."[76]

We should expect the creation and destruction of social capital to be marked by virtuous and vicious cycles. . . . In the absence of trust there can be no certainty in contracts and hence no force to the laws and a society in that condition is effectively reduced to a state of semi-savagery . . . the savages who will only give with the right hand if they simultaneously receive with the left. . . . Networks of civic engagement improve the flow of information about the trustworthiness of individuals . . . embody past success at collaboration . . . increase the potential costs to a defector . . . foster robust norms of reciprocity."[77]

The proposals here constitute an application to the problems of developed nations of methods--the organization of sub-local institutions--that they have freely prescribed and practiced in connection with economic development in underdeveloped countries.[78] Perhaps the appropriate last word is that of Thomas Jefferson:

Begin them only for a single purpose; they will soon show for what other they are the best instruments.[79]

NOTES

1. C. Clarke, *Community Councils: Power to the People?* in *British Political Sociology Yearbook* (C. Cranch ed. 1977), at 110, 125. "Many problems are more efficiently solved at the local level: e.g. crime control, supervision of small children, care of the aged or mentally ill, small crises, and even some economic tasks. For cogent reviews of data, and not merely arguments, see . . . Vol. 1 of A. Inkeles, et al., eds. Annual Review of Sociology (1975)." From W. Goode, *The Celebration of Heroes* (1978), at 392 n.25.

2. J. Elshtain, *Catholic Social Thought, the City, and Liberal America* (1993), at 31 n.14.

3. A. Smith, *The Wealth of Nations*, bk. V, ch. I, pt. III, art. III. For a similar modern observation, see P.Berger, *The Concept of Mediating Action*, in *Confession, Conflict, and Community* (R. Neuhaus ed. 1986), at 4-5.

4. P. Smith, *As a City upon a Hill: The Town in American History* (1968).

5. T. Friedgut, *Political Participation in the USSR* (1979), at 257.

6. P. Melvin, *American Community Organization: A Historical Dictionary* (1986), at 150.

7. Liggett Co. v. Lee (dissenting opinion).

8. L. Mumford, *The City in History* (1961), at 500.

9. M. Baumgartner, *The Moral Order of a Suburb* (1988), at 134-35.

10. G. Sabine, *A History of Political Theory* (1950), at 6.

11. A. Zimmern, *The Greek Commonwealth* (Modern Library ed.) notes that the substitution for a birth qualification for citizenship in English boroughs dates only from 1835.

12. *Id.* at 153-59, describes the demes.

13. *Id.* at 174.

14. Thucydides, *The Pelopensian War*, bk. II (Jowett trans. 1900) at 35-36, quoted in Sabine, *supra* note 10, at 14.

15. Sabine, *supra* note 10, at 141.

16. See E. Barker, *Introduction to Social Contract: Essays by Locke, Hume and Rousseau* 1 (1947); K. Popper, *The Open Society and Its Enemies* (1945).

17. Barker, *supra* note 16, ch 4. Barker notes:

Rousseau himself realized that his theory suited only the small community, such as Greece had known and Switzerland still knew; and he would have reconciled it to the greater size of the modern state either by advocating a moveable metropolis if a state had many towns or by suggesting some system of federalism. . . . Federalism is only mentioned in a single sentence of the Contract Social, but there is a story that Rousseau wrote 16 chapters on the subject, which he entrusted in manuscript to a friend, who destroyed them at the beginning of the French Revolution. (at 111)

As for the significance of small associations, Burke wrote:

To be attached to the subdivision, to love the little platoon we belong to in society, is the first principle (the germ as it were) of public affections. . . . We begin our public connections in families. We pass on to our neighborhoods and our provincial connections. These are our inns and resting places. Such divisions of our country as have been formed by habit and not by a sudden jerk of authority are like so many little images of the great country in which the heart has found something it could fill. The love to the whole is not extinguished by this subordinate particularly.

From E. Burke, *Reflections on the Revolution in France* (Anchor ed. 1973), at 59 quoted in B. Barber, *Strong Democracy: Participatory Politics For a New Age* (1984), at 248. See S. Huntington, *The Founding Fathers and the Division of Powers*, in *Area and Power* (A. Maass ed., 1959), citing Jefferson's letters to John Tyler (5/26/1810); John Adams (10/28/1813); Joseph Cabell (1/17/1814, 1/31/1814, 2/2/1816); Wilson Nicholas (4/2/1816); John Taylor (5/28/1816); James Breckinridge (2/15/1821); John Cartwright (6/5/1824); and Samuel Kerceval (7/2/1816, 9/5/1816).

18. T. Jefferson, 2 *Autobiographical Writings*, at 122.

19. See *id.*

20. Huntington, *supra* note 17. For Jefferson's views on elementary education, see R. Honeywell, *The Educational Work of Thomas Jefferson*, ch. 2, app. A (1931).

21. See e.g., G. Liebmann, *Maryland District Court Law and Practice* (1976), at 1-31: "The Americans have adopted the English system of justices of the peace, depriving it of the aristocratic character that distinguishes it in the mother country." See also A. de Tocqueville, 1 *Democracy in America* (Vintage ed. 1954), at 77.

22. For contemporary discussion of a militia system in Europe, see G. Sharp, *Making Europe Unconquerable* (1985).

23. In many states, constables for small election districts have continued to be appointed until the present time. See, e.g., 52 Opinions of the Attorney General of Maryland 108 (1967).

24. J. Mill, *Representative Government* (Everyman ed.), at 477, 479.

25. J. Mill, *On Liberty* (Everyman ed.), at 222.

26. De Tocqueville, *supra* note 21, at 2: 318-19.

There are countries in Europe where the inhabitant feels like some sort of farm laborer indifferent to the fate of the place where he dwells . . . the condition of his village, the policing of his road, and the repair of his church and parsonage do not concern him; he thinks that all those things have nothing to do with him at all, but belong to a powerful stranger called government.

From *id.*, at vol. 1, 93-94 (quoted in M. Glendon, *Rights Talk* [1991], at 119-20, "It is especially dangerous to enslave men in the minor details of life." From *id.* at 2: 219. See also H. Eckstein, *A Theory of Stable Democracy* (1961): "[A] government will tend to be stable if its authority pattern is congruent with the other authority patterns of the society of which it is a part."

27. J. Schumpeter, 162 *Capitalism, Socialism, and Democracy* (1942), at 239: "[D]ematerialized, defunctionalized and absentee ownership does not impress and call forth moral allegiance as the vital form of property did. Eventually there will be *nobody* left who really cares to stand for it--nobody within or without the precincts of the big concerns."

28. R. Niebuhr, quoted in B. Barber, *Strong Democracy: Participatory Politics for a New Age* (1984), at 139. See also J. Dewey, *The Public and Its Problems* (1946), at 212-15.

29. See W. Whyte, *The Last Landscape* (1968); *idem*, Cluster Zoning (1971).

30. D. Riesman, *Some Observations on Community Plans and Utopia*, 57 Yale Law Journal (1947), reprinted in *Individualism Reconsidered* (Anchor ed. 1955), at 67.

31. P. Ylvisaker, *Criteria for a "Proper" Areal Division of Powers* in *Area and Power* (A. Maass ed., 1959), at 45.

32. C. Mills, *The Power Elite* (1956), at 5. 32. See also R. Unger, *Knowledge and Politics* (1975), with its appeal for a "community of values." The heirs of the Jacobin tradition, with their reliance at worst on revolution, at best on legalism, are subject to Sir Henry Maine's charge, equally applicable to our contemporary civil liberties unions· "The philosophers of France, in their eagerness to escape from what they deemed a superstition of the priests, flung themselves headlong into a superstition of the lawyers." From *Ancient Law* (1885), quoted in N. Glazer, *The Limits of Social Policy* (1991), at 144.

33. S. Weil, *The Need for Roots* (1944), at 15, 16, 123, 162. Compare S. S. Hoffmann, *Areal Division in Writings of French Political Thinkers*, in *Area and Power*, *supra* note 31, at 141: "Centralization, far from being a weapon of social and political integration, carefully perpetuated the centrifugal forces. . . . [T]hese forces, unable to express (and exhaust) themselves in the component areas, infiltrated and contaminated the center itself."

34. H. Arendt, *On Revolution* (1965), at 259.

35. *Id.* at 265-66, quoting F. Jelleneto, *The Paris Commune of 1871*, (1937), at 71.

36. *Id.* at 283. As previously shown, however, Arendt was not accurate in saying: "[O]n one point, however, Jefferson remained curiously silent, and that is the question of what the specific functions of the elementary republics should be." *Id.* at 258.

37. *Id.* at 268. The advantages and disadvantages of direct democracy are ably summarized in R. Dahl and E. Tufte, *Size and Democracy* (1973), at 13-15.

38. R. Nisbet, *Community and Power* (1962), at XV. Nisbet went on:

They appeal to the courts, but not even the American judicial system can remain for very long untouched by the drive toward political uniformity and centralization. They appeal to the rights of man, but except in a religious sense which few liberals take seriously, there are not rights of man which do not proceed from the society in which human beings live.

Id. at 256. Compare Glazer, supra note 32, at 106-7: "We have seen in the U.S. a shift from community organizers . . . dominant in the later 1960's to lawyers, increasingly dominant in the later 1970's and the 1980's. . . . Now the task of participation is in the hands of lawyers operating under the loose provisions of American law which enable a lawyer to represent a huge class and to gain victories for that class, often unbeknownst to most of them."

39. D. Popenoe, *Private Pleasure, Public Plight: American Metropolitan Community Life in Comparative Perspective* (1990), at 133: "Bereft of both private networks and traditional groups the dominant force in this person's life becomes the mass media, especially television and whatever meanings and value these media impart."

40. *Id.* at 157, 154 (referring to C. Perry, *The Neighborhood Unit* [1929]).

41. P. Berger, *Facing Up to Modernity* (1977), at 140; see also Berger, *supra* note 3, at 8-18: "Our argument is not against modernity but in favor of exploring the ways in which modernity can be made more humane." See also E. Richardson, *The Creative Balance* (1976), at 297.

42. R. Dahl and E. Tufte, *Size and Democracy* (1973), at 140.

43. H. Wells, *Mankind in the Making* (1903), Maass, *supra* note 31, at 215.

44. S. Barton and C. Silverman, *The Political Life of Mandatory Homeowner's Associations*, in U.S. Advisory Commission on Intergovernmental Relations, *Residential Community Associations* (1989), at 31, 36.

45. L. Newton, *The Community and the Cattle Pen: An Analysis of Participation*, in *Nomos XVI: Participation in Politics* (J. Pennock et al. eds. 1975), at 233, 244. Newton continues: "All other efforts, if this one has not succeeded, must eventually fail."

46. J. Mansbridge, *The Limits of Friendship*, in *id.*, at 246, 264.

47. J. Pennock and J. Chapman, Preface to *Participation in Politics*, *supra* note 45, at viii. See also P. Drucker, *The End of Economic Man* (1939); Erich Fromm, *Escape From Freedom* (1941).

48. P. Smith, *As a City upon a Hill* (1968), at 305-06.

49. Kaufman, *Administrative Decentralization and Political Power,* 29 Public Administration Review 12 (1969).

50. W. Pfaff, *Condemned to Freedom* (1971), at 167.

51. *Id.* at 194.

52. Much of the literature is summarized in Hollis, *Women and Planning,* 46 Journal of the American Planning Association 456 (1979). See also C. Stimpson, *Women and the American City* (1981); D. Rothblatt, *The Suburban Environment and Women* (1979); K. Hapgood, *Planning, Women and Change* (1974).

53. D. Hayden, *Redesigning the American Dream: The Future of Housing, Work and Family Life* (1984), at 19.

54. The percentage of men never married increased from 17.3% to 25.2% from 1960 to 1985; the corresponding figure for women from 11.9% to 18.2%. See *infra* note 55.

55. The percentage of never-married women between the ages of 25 and 29 increased from 10.5% in 1960 to 26.4% in 1985, U.S. Bureau of the Census, summarized in *The World Almanac and Book of Facts* (1988), at 813.

56. The average number of persons per household declined from 3.14 in 1970 to 2.76 in 1980, 2.69 in 1985, and 2.67 in 1986. The number of persons over 14 living alone increased from 7,064,000 in 1960 to 20,602,000 in 1985. The number of households with six or more persons declined from 6.8 million in 1965 to 3.6 million in 1985.

57. Births to unmarried women as a percentage of all births increased from 3.0% in 1950 to 18.4% in 1980 and 25.7% in 1988. In absolute numbers, there was a sixfold increase in births to unmarried black women and a tenfold increase in births to unmarried white women. National Center for Health Statistics.

58. The number of divorces granted in the United States increased from 385,144 in 1950 to 708,000 in 1970 and 1,175,000 in 1988. *Id.* at 135. As of 1950, 58% of women 65 years of age or older with no spouse present lived with relatives. The percentage declined to 29% by 1970 and 18% by 1980. Shareis, *Older People and Their Families,* 41 Journal of Marriage and the Family 945 (1980).

59. Hayden, *supra* note 53, at 180.

60. *Id.* at 207.

61. V. Gruen, *Heart of Our Cities* (1965), at 107.

62. Hayden, *supra* note 53, at 207.

63. Id. at 180.

64. Id. at 178.

65. *Id.* at 178.

66. *Id.* at 179.

67. *Id.*

68. *Id.* at 183.

69. D. Thorns, *The Quest for Community* (1976), at 62. See also R. Calvan, *Children and Families: The Latent Victims of Exclusionary Zoning Practices*, in *Management and Control of Growth: Updating the Law* (F. Schnidman ed. 1980); M. Glendon, *The Transformation of Family Law: State, Law, and Family in the United States and Europe* (1989), at 308 ("governments might be able to assist families and their members indirectly by attending to the health of surrounding small-scale communities."); S. Rothman, *Woman's Proper Place* (1978), at 271.

70. G. Suttles, *The Defended Neighborhood* (1972) at 249; D. Popenoe, *Suburbanization, Privatization and Juvenile Delinquency: Some Possible Relationships*, in *Housing and Neighborhoods: Theoretical and Empirical Considerations* (W. Van Vliet et al. eds. 1987), at 119-37.

71. C. Rose, *Planning and Dealing*, 71 California Law Review 837, 886-87 (1983). See the proposal for enabling legislation in R. Hawkins, *Neighborhood Policy* in *Neighborhood Policy and Planning* (P. Clay ed. 1983), at 193; see also C. Hatch, *The Scope of Social Architecture* (1984); U.S. Advisory Commission on Intergovernmental Relations, 2 *Fiscal Balance in the American Federal System* (1967), at 16-17 (proposing taxing authority for neighborhoods). See also M. Kotler, *Neighborhood Government* (1969), at 42. The ACIR proposals are in ACIR, *The State and Distressed Communities* (1985), at 245; see also ACIR, *The Organization of Local Public Economies* (1967), at 25-26.

72. H. Simons, *Economic Policy for a Free Society* (1946), at 12.

73. A. Hirschman, *Exit, Voice and Loyalty* (1970), at 108.

74. F. Hayek, 3 *Law, Legislation and Liberty* (1982), at 146.

75. R. Putman, *Making Democracy Work: Civic Culture in Italy* (1993) at 166.

76. *Id.* at 170.

77. *Id.* at 174.

78. See the stress on creation of self-help projects at the sublocal level in United Nations, *Social Progress Through Community Development* (1956); and in C. Taylor, *Community Development Programs and Methods*, 3 Community Development Review 35 (1956); as well as in a vast "community development" literature generated by international aid organizations.

79. Letter to Joseph C. Cabell, 2 February, 1816, in A. Koch and W. Peden, *The Life and Selected Writing of Thomas Jefferson* (1944), at 661-62.

Selected Bibliography

BRITAIN

Abrams, P. *Neighborhood Care and Social Policy.* London: HMSO, 1989.

Adams, R. *Self-Help, Social Work and Empowerment.* London: Macmillan, 1990.

Association of London Authorities. *Tenants in Power: A Radical Alternative to the Government's Public Housing Proposals.* London: Author, 1988.

Audit Commission. *Making Community Care a Reality.* London: HMSO, 1986.

Audit Commission. *Managing the Crisis in Council Housing.* London: HMSO, 1986.

Bauer, C. *Modern Housing.* Boston: Houghton Mifflin, 1934.

Bennett, T. *Evaluating Neighborhood Watch.* London: Gower, 1990.

Brambila, R., et al. *For Pedestrians Only.* New York: Whitney of Design, 1977.

Buchanan, C. *Traffic in Towns.* London: HMSO, 1963.

Bulmer, M. ed. *Neighbors: The Work of Philip Abrams.* Cambridge: Cambridge University Press, 1986.

Bulmer, M. *The Social Basis of Community Care.* London: Allen and Unwin, 1987.

Coleman, A. *Utopia and Committee.* [Seebohn] Report. London: HMSO, 1968.

Coleman, A. Committee on Local Authority and Allied Services. *Utopia on Trial.* London. II. Shipman, 1985.

Crossman, R. *Diaries of a Cabinet Minister.* New York: Holt, 1976.

Crouch, C. ed. *Participation in Politics: British Political Sociology Yearbook.* London: C. Helm, 1977.

Delafons, J. "Conservation See-Saw." 62 *Town and Country Planning* 227 (1993).

Department of Health and Social Security. *Care in the Community.* London: HMSO, 1983.

Department of Health and Social Security. *Caring for People.* (Cm. 849). London: HMSO, 1989.

Department of Health and Social Security. *Community Care: Agenda for Action.* London: HMSO, 1989.

Department of Health and Social Security. *A Happier Old Age.* London: HMSO, 1988.

Department of the Environment. *Crime Prevention on Council Estates*. London: HMSO, 1993.

Department of the Environment. *The Future of Parishes and Neighborhoods*. London: HMSO, 1971.

Department of the Environment. *The Neighborhood Council*. London: HMSO, 1977.

Department of the Environment. *Roles and Activities of Parish and Town Councils in England: Case Studies*. London: HMSO, 1993.

Ensor, R. "Supersession of County Government." *Politica* 425 (1935).

Hall, P. *London 2000*. London: Faber and Faber, 1963.

Hass-Klau, C. "Environmental Traffic Management in Britain: Does It Exist?" 12 *Built Environment* 7 (1986).

Hatch, S. ed. *Toward Participation in Local Services*. London: Fabian Society, 1973.

Hay, D. and Snyder. *Policing and Prosecution in Britain 1750-1850*. Oxford: Clarendon Press, 1988.

Hiller, B. "City of Alice's Dreams." *Architects' Journal*, 9 July 1986, 39.

Home Office. *Community Work and the Probation Service*. London: HMSO, 1991.

Hope, T. and M. Shaw. *Communities and Crime Reduction*. 1990.

House of Commons. *Community Care*. London: HMSO, 1985.

House of Commons. *Community Care Developments*. London: HMSO, 1988.

Jennings, H. *Societies in the Making*. London: Routledge, 1962.

Knight, B. *Self-Help in the Inner City*. London: London Voluntary Service Council, 1981.

Law Commission. *Report on Law of Positive and Restrictive Covenants* (Report 127). London: HMSO, 1989.

Law Commission. *Report on Positive Covenants Affecting Land* (Cmnd. 2719). London: HMSO, 1965.

Lipman, V. *Local Government Areas 1834-1945*. Westport, Conn.: Greenwood Press, 1976; reissue of 1949 ed.

Mabileau, A., et al. *Local Politics and Participation in Britain and France*. Cambridge: Cambridge University Press, 1989.

Ministry of Health. *The Development of Community Care*. London: HMSO, 1973.

Ministry of Housing and Local Government. *The Needs of New Communities*. London: HMSO, 1967.

Morris, M. *Voluntary Work in the Welfare State*. London: Routledge, 1969.

Moudon, A. ed. *Public Streets for Public Use*. New York: Van Nostrand, 1987.

National Audit Office. *Community Care Development*. London: HMSO, 1987.

Payne, S. "Too Conservative a Solution: The Conservation Area Test." 55 *Modern Law Review*. 726 (1992).

Prest, J. *Liberty and Locality: Parliament, Permissive Legislation and Ratepayer Democracies in the Nineteenth Century*. Oxford: Clarendon Press, 1990.

Pringle, P. *Hue and Cry*. New York: William Morrow, 1969.

Redlich, J. and Hirst. *Local Government in England*. London: Macmillan, 1903.

Rees, I. *Government by Community*. London: C. Knight, 1971.

Royal Commission on Distribution of Industrial Population. *Report* (Cmd. 6153). London: HMSO, 1940.

Royal Commission on Local Government in England. *Report* Cmnd. 4040. London: HMSO, 1969.

Royal Commission on Local Government in England. *Written Evidence*. London: HMSO, 1969.

Scottish Department. *The Structure of Scottish Local Government: Shaping the Future: The New Councils* (Cm. 2267). London: HMSO, 1993.

Scottish Development Council. *Community Councils*. London: HMSO, 1974.

Scottish Development Department. *Report of Morris Committee on Links Between Housing and Social Work*. London: HMSO, 1975.

Scottish Housing Advisory Comittee. *Council House Communities*. London: HMSO, 1970.

Sharp, E. "Parish Pump in the 70's." *Manchester Guardian* 10 (19 December 1969).

Stringer, P. "A Comparison of Parish Councils and Voluntary Organizations in Action." 10 *Journal of Voluntary Action Research* 62 (1981).

Sutcliffe, A. *Multi-Story Living*. London: Croom Helm, 1974.

Taylor, N. *The Village in the City*. London: Temple Smith, 1973.

Ward, P. ed. *Conservation and Development in Historic Towns and Cities*. York: University of York, 1968.

Ward, R. *The Process of Local Government Reform, 1966-74*. London: Allen and Unwin, 1976.

Webb, S. and B. Webb. *Constitution for the Socialist Commonwealth of Great Britain*. Cambridge: 3d ed. Cambridge University Press, 1975.

Webb, S. and B. Webb. *Development of English Local Government, 1689-1835*. Oxford: Oxford University Press, 1963.

Webb, S. and B. Webb. *English Local Government: The Old Poor Law*. London: Archon Books, 1963; reprint of 1927 ed.

Webb, S. and B. Webb. *English Local Government: The Parish and the County*. London: Archon Books, 1963; reprint of 1906 ed.

Webb, S. and B. Webb. *English Local Government: The Story of the King's Highway*. London: Archon Books, 1963; reprint of 1920 ed.

Welsh Department. *Local Government in Wales: A Charter for the Future* (Cm. 2155). London: HMSO, March 1993.

Wilson, P. *Trends and Issues in Crime and Criminal Justice*. 1990.

Wright, A. *Citizens and Subjects: An Essay on British Politics*. 1994.

FRANCE

Ardagh, J. *France in the 1980's*. London: Secker and Warburg, 1982.

Ardagh, J. *France Today*. London: Secker and Warburg, 1987.

Batley, R., et al. *Local Government in Europe: Trends and Developments*. New York: St. Martin's Press, 1991.

Booth, P. *Decision Making and Decentralization: Development Control in France*. Sheffield: University of Sheffield Department of Town and Regional Planning, 1985.

Brown. "F1rench Co-Property of Apartments." 110 *Solicitors Journal* 630 (1966).

Bullock, N. and J. Read. *Movement for Housing Reform in Germany and France 1840-1914*. Cambridge: Cambridge University Press, 1985.

Cerny, P. ed. *Socialism, the State, and Public Policy*. London: Methuen, 1985.

Clarke, S. ed. *Urban Innovation and Autonomy*. New York: Sage Publications, 1989.

Cornford, J. ed. *The Failure of the State. London: Croom Helm*, 1975.

Crouch, C. *The New Centralism*. Oxford: Blackwell, 1989.

de Gaulle, C. *Memoirs of Hope: Renewal and Endeavor*. New York: Simon and Schuster, 1971.

Dyson, H. *French Real Property and Succession Law*. 2d ed. 1991.

Flockton. C. "French Local Government Reform and Urban Planning." 9 *Local Government Studies* (N.S.) 65 (1983).

Garrish, S. *Centralization and Decentralization in England and France*. Bristol: University of Bristol School for Advanced Urban Studies, 1986.

Gourevitch, P. *Paris and the Provinces: The Politics of Local Government Reform in France*. Berkeley: University of California Press, 1980.

Grew, R., et al., eds. *Crises of Political Development in Europe and the United States*. Princeton: Princeton University Press, 1978.

Hill, J. "Freehold Flats in French Law," *Conveyancer and Property Lawyer* (N.S.) 337 (1985).

Kain, R. "Europe's Model and Exemplar Still? The French Approach to Urban Conservation, 1962-1981." 53 *Town Planning Review* 403 (1982).

Keating, M. and P. Hainesworth. *Decentralizationand Change in Contemporary France*. London: Gower, 1986.

Le Gales, P. "New Directions in Decentralization and Urban Policy in France." 10 *Environment and Planning* (1992).

Levine, A. "The Transformation of Urban Politics in France." 29 *Urban Affairs Quarterly* 383 (1994).

Mabileau, A., et al. *Local Politics and Participation in Britain and France*. Cambridge: Cambridge University Press, 1989.

Peyrefitle, A. *Le Mal Francais*. Paris: Plon, 1976.

Pugsley. "French Local Authority Meetings," *Local Governmnt Review* 18 (September 1982).

Punter, J. "Planning Control in France." 59 *Town Planning Review* 159 (1988).

Ridley, F. and J. Blondel. *Public Administrationin France*. New York: Barnes and Noble, 2d ed. 1969.

Ross, G. ed. *The Mitterand Experiment*. London: Polity, 1987.

Safran, W. *The French Polity*. 2d ed. London: Longman, 1985.

Schmidt, V. *Democraticizing France*. Cambridge: Cambridge University Press, 1990.

Schmidt, V. "Unblocking Politics by Decree." 22 *Comparative Politics* 459 (1990).

Shankland, Cox and Associates. *La vie dans un grand ensemble*. London: Shankland, Cox and Associates, 1971.

Tupper, I. and P. Mingret. "Suburban Malaise in French Cities." 57 *Town Planning Review* 194 (1986).

Wilson, I. "The Preparation of Local Plans in France." 54 *Town Planning Review* 172 (1959).

Wright, V. and H. Machin. "The French Regional Reform of July 1972: A Case of Disguised Centralization." 3 *Policy and Politics* 3 (1975).

Zeldin, T. *France 1848-1945*. Oxford: Clarendon Press, 1977.

GERMANY

Barnes, P. "Environmental Traffic Restraint: German Approaches to Traffic Management by Design." 12 *Built Environment* 60 (1986).

Bullock, N. and J. Read. *Movement for Housing Reform in Germany and France 1840-1914*. Cambridge: Cambridge University Press, 1985.

Dawson, W. *Municipal Life and Government in Germany*. London: Longman's, 1914.

Greene, E. "West German City Reconstruction: Two Case Studies," 7 *Social Review* (N S.) 231 (1959).

Gunlicks, A. *Local Government in the German Federal System*. Durham, NC: Duke University Press, 1986.

Hass-Klau, C. "Soft Urban Renewal in Krenzburz." 12 *Built Environment* 165 (1986).

Hass-Klau, C. *The Pedestrian and City Traffic*. London: Belhaven Press, 1990.

Hiscocks, R. *Democracy in Western Germany*. Oxford: Oxford University Press, 1957.

Hooper, A. "Development Control in the Federal Republic of Germany." 59 *Town Planning Review* 198 (1988).

Howe, F. *European Cities at Work*. New York: Scribner, 1913.

Kimminich, O. "Public Participation in the Federal Republic of Germany." 53 *Town Planning Review* 274 (1982).

Kube, E. ed. *Police Research in the Federal Republic of Germany*. Berlin: Springer-Verlag, 1991.

Lehmann, H. *American Policy and the Reconstruction of West Germany, 1945-55*. New York: Oxford University Press, 1993.

Lunn, H. *Municipal Lessons from Southern Germany*. 1908.

Melnecke, F. *The Age of German Liberation, 1795-1815*. Berkeley: University of California Press, 1977.

Moudon, A. ed. *Public Streets for Public Use* New York: Van Nostrand, 1987.

Norton, A. ed. *Present and Future Role of Local Government in Great Britain and the Federal Republic of Germany*. Birmingham: University of Birmingham, 1985.

Organization for Economic Cooperation and Development. *Traffic Safety in Residential Areas*. Paris: OECD, 1979.

Pharaoh, T. and J. Russell.. "Traffic Calming Policy and Performance: The Netherlands, Denmark and Germany." 62 *Town Planning Review* 79 (1991).

Robson, W. "Local Government in Occupied Germany." 16 *Political Quarterly* 277 (1945).

Robson, W. *Great Cities of the World*. 2d ed. New York: Macmillan, 1957.

Russell, J. "Viewpoint: Traffic Calming and Town Planning." 61 *Town Planning Review* iii (1990).

Schoenbrun, T. "Planning and Land Development Law in the Federal Republic of Germany." 54 *Tulane Law Review* 624 (1980).

Schweitzer, C., et al. *Politics and Government in the Federal Republic of Germany: Basic Documents.* New York: St. Martin's Press, 1984.

Seeley, J. *Life and Times of Stein.* Vol. 2. Cambridge: Cambridge University Press, 1878.

Walker, M. *German Home Towns: Community, State and General Estate, 1648-1871.* Ithaca, N.Y.: Cornell University Press, 1971.

Weinberger, B. "Local Government Taxes in Germany and Their Future." 3 *Studies in Comparative Local Government* no. 2 (1969).

THE UNITED STATES

Adams, H. *Norman Constables in America.* Baltimore: Johns Hopkins University, 1883.

American Law Institute, *Restatement of Property: Servitudes.* Philadelphia: American Law Institute, 1992-94.

Babcock, R., et al. *Special Districts: The Ultimate in Neighborhood Zoning.* Cambridge, Mass: Lincoln Institute for Land Policy, 1990.

Barber, B. *Strong Democracy.* Berkeley: University of California Press, 1984.

Baumgartner, M. *The Moral Order of a Suburb.* Oxford: Oxford University Press, 1988.

Berger, P. *Facing Up to Modernity.* New York: Basic Books, 1977.

Berger, P. and R. Neuhaus. *To Empower People.* Washington, D.C.: American Enterprise Institute, 1977.

Caftel, B. *Community Development Credit Unions.* 1978.

Campbell-Hall, D. "Homeowners Association-Is Tax Exemption Worth the Effort." 20 *Real Prop. Probate and Trust Journal* 647 (1955).

Clay, P. and Hollister, eds. *Neighborhood Policy and Planning.* New York: Lexington Books, 1983.

Cohen, A. "Zoning for Family Day Care." In *Zoning and Planning Law Handbook,* K. Young ed. New York: Clark, Boardman & Co., 1991.

Cunningham, J. *The Resurgent Neighborhood.* Notre Dame, Ind.: Fides Publishers, 1965.

Dahl, R., et al. *Size and Democracy.* Palo Alto, Cal.: Stanford University Press, 1973.

Danzig, D. "Toward the Creation of a Complementary Decentralized System of Criminal Justice." 26 *Stanford Law Review* 1 (1973).

Dewey, R. "The Neighborhood, Urban Ecology and City Planners." 15 *American Sociological Review* 502 (1950).

Diamond, S. "Death and Transfiguration of Benefit Taxation." 12 *Journal of Legal Studies* 202 (1983).

Dillich, S. *Community Organization for Neighborhood Development.* New York: W. Morrow, 1953.

Dillon, J. *Treatise on the Law and Municipal Corporations.* Chicago: James Cockcroft, 1872.

Eldridge, S. "Community Organization and Citizenship." 7 *Social Forces* 140 (1921).

Ellichson, R. "Alternatives to Zoning." 40 *University of Chicago Law Review* 681 (1973).

Epstein, R. "Covenants and Constitutions." 73 *Cornell Law Review* 906 (1988).

Faher, C. "Is Local Control of Schools Still a Viable Option?" 14 *Harvard Journal of Law and Public Policy* 447 (1991).

Farr, W., et al. *Decentralizing City Government: A Practical Study of a Radical Proposal for New York City.* New York: Lexington Books, 1977.

Fischel, W. *The Economics of Zoning Laws.* Baltimore: Johns Hopkins University Press, 1985.

Follett, M. *The New State.* London: Longman's, 1934.

Frederickson, G. "Recovery of Civism in Public Administration." 41 *Public Administration Review.* 501 (1981).

Freund, F. "Some Inadequately Discussed Problems of the Law of Zoning." In *Planning Problems of Town, City and Region.* Philadelphia: Wm. F. Fell Co., 1929).

Frug, J. "The City as a Legal Concept." 93 *Harvard Law Review* 4 (1979).

Geisler, C. ed. *Land Reform: American Style.* Totawa, N.J.: Rowman and Allanheld, 1984.

Gillette, C. "In Partial Praise of Dillon's Rule." 67 *Chi-Kent Law Review* 959 (1991).

Glueck, E. *Community Use of Schools.* Baltimore: Williams, 1927.

Gottdiener, M. *Planned Sprawl.* New York: Sage Publications, 1977.

Gruen, V. *Heart of Our Cities.* New York: Simon and Schuster, 1964.

Haar, C., et al., eds. *Zoning and the American Dream.* Cambridge, Mass · Lincoln Institute of Land Policy, 1989.

Hagman, D. and Miscynski. *Windfalls for Wipeouts.* Chicago: Planners' Press, 1978.

Hallman, H. *Neighborhoods, Their Place in Urban Life.* New York: Sage Publications, 1984.

Hartog, J. *Public Property and Private Power: The Corporation of the City of New York in American Law, 1730-1870.* Chapel Hill: University of North Carolina Press, 1983.

Hawkins, R. *Self-Government by District.* Palo Alto, Cal.: Hoover Institution Press, 1976.

Hayden, D. *Redesigning the American Dream: The Future of Housing, Work and Family Life.* New York: W.W. Norton, 1984.

Henderson, J. "Community Development: The Effects of Growth and Uncertainty." 70 *Amer. Econ. Rev.* 894 (1980).

Hess, K. *Community Technology.* New York: Harper and Row, 1979.

Hester, R. *Neighborhood Space.* New York: Halsted Press, 1985.

Hollis, C. "Women and Planning." 46 *Journal of the American Planning Association* 456 (1979).

Honeywell, R. ed. *The Educational Work of Thomas Jefferson.* Cambridge, Mass.: Harvard University Press, 1931.

Hyatt, W. *Community Association Law.* 2d ed. Philadelphia: American Law Institute, American Bar Association Committee on Continuing Professional Education, 1988.

Inkeles, A., et al. *Annual Review of Sociology.* Vol. 1. Palo Alto, Cal.: Annual Reviews, Inc., 1975.

Isaac, R. "The Neighborhood Theory: An Analysis of Its Adequacy." 14 *Journal of the American Planning Association* 15 (1948).

Janowitz, M. *The Community Press in an Urban Setting.* Chicago: Univeristy of Chicago Press, 1952.

Kotler, M. *Neighborhood Government: The Local Foundation of Political Life.* Indianapolis: Bobbs Merrill, 1969.

Kristol, I. "Decentralization for What?" 11 *Public Interest* 9 (1968).

Levine, C. "Citizenship and Service Delivery." 44 *Public Administration Review* 78 (1984).

Liebmann, G. "Delegation to Private Parties in American Constitutional Law." 50 *Indiana Law Journal* 650 (1975).

Liebmann, G. "Suburban Zoning: Two Modest Proposals." 25 *Real Property, Probate and Trust Journal* 1 (1991).

Lowrie, S. "The Social Unit: An Experiment in Politics." 9 *National Municipal Review* 553 (1923).

Maass, A. ed. *Area and Power.* Glencoe, Ill. Free Press, 1959.

Mansbridge, J. *Beyond Adversary Democracy.* New York: Basic Books, 1980.

McBain, H. "Law Making by Property Owners." 36 *Political Science Quarterly* 167 (1921).

Melvin, P. *American Community Organization: A Historical Dictionary.* New York: Greenwood, 1986.

Michelman, F. "Law's Republic." 97 *Yale Law Journal* 1493 (1988).

Monti, D. "Organization, Strengths and Weaknesses of Resident-Managed Public Housing Sites in the U.S." 11 *Journal of Urban Affairs* 1 (1989).

Morris, T., et al. *Neighborhood Power: The New Localism.* Boston: Beacon Press, 1975.

Moynihan, D. *Maximum Feasible Misunderstanding: Community Action in the War on Poverty.* Glencoe, Ill: Free Press, 1969.

Mumford, L. "The Neighborhood and the Neighborhood Unit." 24 *Town Planning Review* 256 (1954).

Nelson, R. "Marketable Zoning." In *Land Use Law and Zoning Digest.* Chicago: American Planning Association, 1985.

Newman, O. *Communities of Interest.* New York: Doubleday, 1972.

Nisbet, R. *Community and Power.* Oxford: Oxford University Press, 1962.

Note. "The Law and Private Streets." 5 *St. Louis University Law Journal* 588 (1954).

Note. "Judicial Review of Condominium Rulemaking." 94 *Harvard Law Review* 647 (1981).

Note. "Historic Districts: Preserving City Neighborhoods for the Privileged." 60 *New York University Law Review* 64 (1985).

Note. "The Rule of Law in Residential Associations." 99 *Harvard Law Review* 472 (1985).

Pancoast, O., et al. *Rediscovering Self-Help: Its Role in Social Care.* New York: Sage Publications, 1983.

Peck, M. *Independent Special Districts.* Ann Arbor, Mich.: University of Michigan Law School, 1962.

Perry, C. *The Neighborhood Unit.* 1929.

Phillips, W. *Adventuring for Democracy.* New York: Social Unit Press, 1940.

Rasmussen, S. "Neighborhood Planning." 27 *Town Planning Review* 197 (1957).

Reichman, U. "Residential Private Governments." 43 *University of Chicago Law Review* 253 (1976).

Richardson, E. "Significant Individual Participation: The New Challenge in American Government." 15 *University of Chicago Law School Record* no. 2 (1967).

Richardson, E. *The Creative Balance*. New York: Holt, 1976.

Rohan, P. *Real Estate Transactions: Homeowner Associations and PUDS*. New York: Matthew Bender, 1988.

Rose, C. "Preservation and Community." 33 *Stanford Law Review*. 473 (1981).

Rose, C. "Planning and Dealing." 71 *California Law Review* 837 (1983).

Rothblatt, D. *The Suburban Environment and Women*. New York: Praeger, 1979.

Rothman, S. *Woman's Proper Place*. New York: Basic Books, 1978.

Schnidman, F. ed. *Management and Control of Growth: Updating the Law*. Washington, D.C.: Urban Law Institute, 1980.

Siegan, B. *Land Use Without Zoning*. New York: Lexington Books, 1972.

Smith, P. *As a City upon a Hill: The Town in American History*. New York: Knopf, 1966.

Steiner, J. ed. *Community Organization*. New York: Century, 1925.

Stimpson, C. *Women and the American City*. Chicago: University of Chicago Press, 1981.

Stokes, B. *Local Responses to Global Problems*. Washington, D.C.: Worldwatch Institute, 1978.

Taylor, L. *Urban Open Space*. New York: Cooper-Hewitt Museum, 1979.

Taylor, R. "Block Crime and Fear." 21 *Journal of Research in Crime and Delinquency* 303, 1984.

Thorns, D. *The Quest for Community*. London: Allen and Unwin, 1976.

Tiebout, J. "A Pure Theory of Local Expenditures." 64 *Journal of Political Economy* 416 (1956).

Trust for Public Land. Neighborhood Land Revitalization Manual. Washington, D.C.: GPO, 1981.

U.S. Advisory Commission on Intergovernmental Relations. *Fiscal Balance in the American Federal System*. Washington, D.C.: GPO, 1983.

U.S. Advisory Commission on Intergovernmental Relations. *Neighborhood Improvement Association and Organization Act*. Washington, D.C.: GPO, 1984.

U.S. Advisory Commission on Intergovernmental Relations. *Cumulative ACIR State Legislative Program: Neighborhood Subunits of Government*. Washington, D.C.: GPO, 1979.

U.S. Advisory Commission on Intergovernmental Relations. *Residential Community Associations: Private Governments in the Intergovernmental System*. Washington, D.C.: GPO 1989.

U.S. Advisory Commission on Intergovernmental Relations. *The State and Distressed Communities*. Washington, D.C.: GPO, 1985.

U.S. Bureau of Education. *Proposed Community Forum Bill*. Washington, D.C.: GPO, 1922.

U.S. Federal Housing Association. *Planned Unit Development with a Homes Association*. Washington, D.C.: GPO, 1963.

Vickery, R. *Anthrophysical Form: Two Families and their Neighborhood Environments*. Charlottesville: University Press of Virginia, 1972.

Warner, S. *The Urban Wildnerness*. New York: Harper and Row, 1972.

Whitaker, G. "Co-Producion: Citizen Participation in Service Delivery." 40 *Public Administration Review* 240 (1990).

White, E. "Community Centers in School Buildings." 1923 *National Conference on Social Work* 40 (1923).

Wood, R. *Suburbia: Its People and Their Politics.* Boston: Houghton Mifflin, 1959.

Woodson, R. *A Summons to Life.* Cambridge, Mass.: Ballinger, 1981.

Yates, D. *Neighborhood Democracy.* New York: Lexington Books, 1973.

Yin, R. *Citizen Organizations: Increasing Client Control over Services.* Santa Monica, Cal.: Rand Corporation, 1973.

Ziegler, E. "State Abrogation of Private Covenants." In *1991 Zoning and Planning Handbook.* K. Young ed. New York: Clark, Boardman & Co. 1991.

Zimmerman, T. *The Federated City: Community Control in Large Cities.* New York: St. Martin's Press, 1972.

CHINA

Brady, F. *Justice and Politics in People's China.* San Diego: Academic Press, 1982.

Buck, D. *Urban Change in China.* Madison: University of Wisconsin Press, 1978.

Cheng Gang. "The Neighborhood Committee: Residents' Own Organization." 33 *Beijing Review* 30 (9 April 1990).

Danguing, R., et al. "Social Networks of Residents in Tianjan with a Comparison to Social Networks in America." 11 *Social Sciences in China* 68 (1990).

Lewis, T. ed. *The City in Communist China.* Palo Alto, Cal.: Stanford University Press, 1971.

Liang, X. "Commercialization of Dwellings and Socialist Practice." 7 *Social Science in China* 77 (1986).

Liebenthal, R. *Revolution and Tradition in Tientsin.* Palo Alto, Cal.: Stanford University Press, 1980.

Lim-Keah, C. *Social Change and the Chinese.* Singapore: Singapore University Press, 1985.

McCormick, B. *Political Reform in Post-Mao China.* Berkeley: University of California Press, 1990.

Shue, V. *The Reach of the State: Sketches of the Chinese Body Politic.* Palo Alto: Stanford University Press, 1988.

Tan, T. "Political Modernization and the Traditional Chinese Voluntary Associations." 13 *Southeast Asian Journal of Social Sciences* 67 (1985).

Tan, T. "Voluntary Associations as a Model of Social Change." 14 *Southeast Asian Journal of Social Sciences* 68 (1986).

Treadgold, D. *Soviet and Chinese Communism.* Seattle: University of Washington Press, 1967.

Vogel, E. *Canton Under Communism.* Cambridge, Mass.: Harvard University Press, 1969.

Whyte, M. *Urban Life in Contemporary China.* Chicago: University of Chicago Press, 1984.

RUSSIA

Andrusz, G. *Housing and Urban Development in the USSR.* Albany: State University of New York Press, 1984.

Berman, H. and Spindler. "Soviet Comrades' Courts." 38 *Washington University Law Review* (1963).

Black, C., et al. *The Modernization of Japan and Russia: A Comparative Study.* Glencoe, Ill: The Free Press, 1975.

Boiter, R. "Comradely Justice: How Durable Is It?" 14 *Problems of Communism* 82 (1965).

DiMaio, A. *Soviet Urban Housing.* New York: Praeger, 1974.

Ellickson, R. "Property in Land," 102 *Yale Law Journal* 1315 (1993).

Friedgut, T. *Political Participation in the USSR.* Princeton, N.J.: Princeton University Press, 1979.

Hahn, J. *Soviet Grassroots: Citizen Participation in Local Soviet Government.* Princeton, N.J.: Princeton University Press, 1988.

Jacobs, E., ed. *Soviet Local Politics and Government.* London: Allen and Unwin, 1983.

Lvov, A. *The Courtyard.* New York: Doubleday, 1989.

Odom, W. *The Soviet Volunteers.* Princeton, N.J.: Princeton University Press, 1974.

Osborn, R. *Soviet Social Policies.* Homewood, Ill.: Dorsey Press, 1970.

Treadgold, D. ed. *Soviet and Chinese Communism: Similarities and Differences.* Seattle: University of Washington Press, 1967.

Unger, A. "Soviet Mass Political Work in Residential Areas." 22 *Soviet Studies* 556 (1970).

Urban, M. *More Power to the Soviets: The Democratic Revolution in the USSR.* London: Gower, 1990.

Wesson, R. "Volunteers and Soviets." 15 *Soviet Studies* 231 (1963).

JAPAN

Ames, W. *Police and Community in Japan.* Berkeley: University of California Press, 1981.

Bayley, D. *Forces of Order: Police Behavior in Japan and the United States.* Berkeley: University of California Press, 1973.

Beardsley, R., et al. *Village Japan.* Chicago: University of Chicago Press, 1959.

Ben-Ari, E. *Changing Japanese Suburbia.* London: Routledge, 1991.

Bestor, T. "Tradition and Japanese Social Organization: Institutional Development in a Tokyo Neighborhood." 24 *Ethnology* 121 (1985).

Black, C. *The Modernization of Japan and Russia.* Glencoe, Ill.: Free Press, 1975.

Braibanti, R. "Neighborhood Associations in Japan and Their Democratic Potentialities." 7 *Far Eastern Quarterly.* 139 (1948).

Campbell, T. "The Old People Boom and Japanese Policymaking." 5 *Journal of Japanese Studies* 21 (1974).

Coaldrake, W. "The Architecture of Reality: Trends in Japanese Housing 1985-89." *Japan Architect* (October 1989).

Dore, W. *City Life in Japan*. Berkeley: University of California Press, 1958.

Ernst, A. "A Segmented Welfare State." 138 *Journal of Institutional and Theoretical Economics* 545 (1982).

Fukutake, T. *Japanese Rural Society*. Ithaca, N.Y.: Cornell University Press, 1967.

Fukutake, T. *The Japanese Social Structure: Its Evolution in the Modern Century*. Tokyo: University of Tokyo Press, 1982.

Garon, S. "The Imperial Bureaucracy and Labor Policy in Post-War Japan." *Journal of Asian Studies* 442 (1984).

Isomura, E., et al. "Recent Trends of Urban Sociology in Japan." 10 *Sociological Review Monograph* 127 (1966).

Koschman, T. ed. *Authority and the Individual in Japan* Tokyo: University of Tokyo Press, 1978.

Linhart, S. "The Search for Meaning in Old Age: The Japanese Case." 12 *International Congress of Gerontology* (1981).

Maeda, D. "Decline of Family Love and the Development of Public Services." In *An Aging World: Dilemmas and Challenges for Law and Social Policy*. J. Eekelaar et al. ed. Oxford: Clarendon Press, 1989.

Masland, J. "Neighborhood Associations in Japan." 15 *Far Eastern Survey* 355 (1948).

Norbeck, E. "Japanese Common Interest Associations in Cross-Cultural Perspective." 1 Journal of *Voluntary Action Scholars* 38 (1972).

SCAP. *Political Reorientation of Japan*. St. Clair Shores, Mich.: Scholarly Press, 1968.

Smith, T. *The Agrarian Origins of Modern Japan*. Palo Alto, Cal.: Stanford University Press, 1959.

Steiner, K. *Local Government in Japan*. Palo Alto, Cal.: Stanford University Press, 1965.

Von Wolfern, K. *The Enigma of Japanese Power*. New York: Knopf, 1989.

Ward, R. "Socio-Political Role of the Boraka in Japan." 45 *American Political Science Review* 1025 (1957).

Warp, G. "In Our Image and Likeness." 42 *National Municipal Review* 176 (1957).

Westey, D. "The Emulation of Western Organizations in Meiji Japan: The Case of the Paris Prefecture of Police." 1984 *Journal of Japanese Studies* 315 (1984).

GENERAL

Anderson, S. *On Streets*. Cambridge, Mass: MIT Press, 1978.

Appleyard, D. ed. *The Conservation of European Cities*. Cambridge, Mass.: MIT Press, 1974.

Appleyard, D. *Liveable Urban Streets*. Washington, D.C.: GPO, 1970.

Cooke T., et al. *Participatory Democracy*. San Francisco: Canfield Press, 1971.

Glendon, M. *The Transformation of Family Law: State Law and Family in the United States and Europe*. Chicago: University of Chicago Press, 1989.

Hirschman, A. *Exit, Voice and Loyalty.* Cambridge: Harvard University Press, 1970.

Jacobs, J. *The Economy of Cities.* New York: Vintage, 1969.

Kray, J. "Woonerven and Other Experiments in the Netherlands." 12 *Built Environment* 20 (1986).

Lefcoe, G. *Land Development in Crowded Places: Lessons from Abroad.* Washington, D.C.: Conservation Foundation, 1979.

Levin, L. "Self Care: An International Perspective." 7 *Social Policy* 70 (1976).

Morlan, R. "Sub-Municipal Government in Practice: The Rotterdam Experience." 35 *Western Political Quarterly* 425 (1982).

Moudon, A. ed. *Pubic Streets for Pubic Use.* New York: Van Nostrand, 1987.

Mumford, L. *The City in History.* New York: Harcourt Brace, 1961.

Nanetti, R. "From the Top Down: Government-Promoted Citizen Participation." 9 *Journal of Volunteer Action Research* 149 (1980).

Pfaff, W. *Condemned to Freedom.* New York: Random House, 1971.

Popenoe, D. *Private Pleasure, Public Plight: American Metropolitan Community Life in Comparative Perspective.* New Brunswick, N.J.: Transaction Books, 1985.

Putnam, R. *Making Democracy Work: Civic Traditions in Modern Italy.* Princeton, N.J.: Princeton University Press, 1993.

Riesenberg, P. *Citizenship in the Western Tradition.* Chapel Hill: University of North Carolina Press, 1992.

Robson, W. *Great Cities.* 2d ed. London: Allen and Unwin, 1957.

Sharp, G. *Making Europe Unconquerable.* Cambridge Mass.: Ballinger, 1985.

Slack, J. "Community Leagues: A Canadian Concept for the Delivery of Municipal Services." 10 *Local Government Studies* (N.S.) 21 (1984).

Susskind, L. *Paternalism, Conflict, and Co-Production, Learning From Citizen Action and Citizen Participation in Western Europe.* New York: Plenum Press, 1983.

United Nations. *Social Progress Through Community Development.* New York: United Nations, 1955.

Van Vliet, W., et al., eds. *Housing and Neighborhoods: Theoretical and Empirical Considerations.* Westport, Conn.: Greenwood Press, 1987.

Name Index

Subject Index

About the Author

GEORGE W. LIEBMANN, an attorney in private practice in Baltimore, Maryland, is a graduate of Dartmouth College and the University of Chicago School of Law. He has served as executive assistant to the Governor of Maryland and Assistant Attorney General of Maryland, and he has taught at Johns Hopkins University and the University of Maryland School of Law. In 1993–94, while writing this book, Liebmann was a Simon Industrial and Professional Fellow at the University of Manchester in England.

ISBN 0-275-95178-2

90000>

EAN

9 780275 951788

HARDCOVER BAR CODE